The
Quotable
Cyclist

Great Moments of Bicycling
Wisdom,
Inspiration
and Humor

Edited by Bill Strickland

BREAKAWAY BOOKS
NEW YORK CITY
1997

THE QUOTABLE CYCLIST:
Great Moments of Bicycling Wisdom, Inspiration and Humor

Compilation copyright © 1997 by Bill Strickland
Introduction and chapter essays copyright © 1997 by Bill Strickland
Photos © by Rich Etchberger, except where otherwise noted.

Quotes from *Training for Cycling*, © Davis Phinney and Connie Carpenter, are
used by kind permission of Penguin Putnam Inc.

ISBN: 1-55821-563-8
Library of Congress Catalog Card Number: 97-70460

Published by BREAKAWAY BOOKS
P.O. Box 24
Halcottsville, NY 12438
(800) 548-4348
(212) 898-0408
Visit our website at **www.breakawaybooks.com**

Distributed by Consortium Book Sales & Distribution

SECOND EDITION

CONTENTS

Thanks, mom, for making it all possible. And never enough thanks to Beth, my wife, the love of my life, who helped me quit my job and become a writer.

ACKNOWLEDGEMENTS

Thanks . . .

. . . whomever you were, for inventing the wheel. And to Leonardo for imagining the bicycle, and Pierre Lallement for making the thing. And the long line from Major Taylor to John Tomac to Lance Armstrong, for showing us how the thing should be ridden. And everyone who has ever ridden a bicycle and said something about it that someone else repeated or wrote down—this really couldn't have happened without you.

. . . Johnny Perez, the closest thing I have to a lifelong friend, for reintroducing me to this wonderful machine after I'd forgotten it and was on the way to what I thought were the things of man. And to the twisted guys I used to wrench with who would drop acid on the job because they loved cycling more than life but more than they loved cycling they hated assembling Strawberry Shortcake bikes. I'm not sure what, and I'm not sure if it was good, but your anti-passion taught me something.

. . . to my homeys at *Mountain Bike* simply for being cool and remembering what it's all about, and Nels for giving me the flexibility to finish this thing. And *Bicycling* magazine for opening its library of ancient cycling magazines and books to me, especially Ed, the big engine who can, and Z, who is the rarest kind of person who always knows when it's time for a good singletrack ride *and* where I can find Raymond Poulidor's palmares.

. . . Tim Blumenthal, who taught me that half the fun of a good mountain bike ride is getting lost, and to stop and dare to eat a peach and look at things (I can almost see the PP&L building and the Appalachian Trail as I write), and to not fret over breakdowns—lessons that served me well putting together this book.

. . . Rich Etchberger, one of the best cycling photographers in the world, and Steven L. Sheffield, the world's first non-fiction domestique, whose work on the bio notes was the equivalent of a long pull back to the peloton. Also thanks to my personal editor, Beth, and my assistants Soren and Lucy. And lanterne rouge but not least, Garth Battista, publisher of Breakaway Books, who always knows how to be there with an encouraging word, just the right insight, and extra days tacked on the back of a deadline.

It's time for a ride.

PROLOGUE

"Anyone who survives the start deserves a medal.
It's crazy."
—**Matt Smith,** mountain bike racer

All my life I've searched for ways to explain to the real world what cycling means to people like you and me. All my life I've failed. First came incoherent, whooping words of pure joy as I almost accidentally discovered the exquisite flight that comes when you finally combine balance and self-propulsion. There were the awkward words of an adolescent wearing funny wool shorts and trying vainly—in both senses of the word—to convince a parade of teenaged girls that bikes were cooler than cars. There were the financial negotiations with confused, angry parents after I spent a summer carrying bricks up scaffoldings to earn tuition money then blew everything I had on a Schwinn Paramount. Just last year I found myself fumbling for the right words to show my uncle the deep flaw in his question: When would I be done with cycling and start writing about something?

And all the times in between, probably much like all your times. A writing (not riding) mentor once told me that no matter what, I should never try to describe a sunset or an orgasm—because neither can ever be as vivid or satisfying as the real deal. When I try to express the beauty and spirituality and grace of cycling I sound like a guy hosting an infomercial for sunsets.

When I began this book, I imagined it as a way for us to reach across the gap, to touch the other side and let them know how it felt to be one of us. I imagined that the sheer scope of the project—love, hate, speed, adventure, disaster, glory, desire, freedom and all the rest—would be enough to build the impossible bridge. That might happen, you know, and it would be nice. But—as isn't uncommon on a long ride—after this one started something became more important than the original intent.

These nine hundred-plus quotes—from more than four hundred pro and amateur racers, recreational riders, writers, mechanics, poets, politicians, scientists, coaches, actors, philosophers and even a few real people (as I once heard noncyclists described)—form a kind of communion for the initiated . . . a celebration and a love song to cycling greater than any single person could create alone. It's all in here in this chorus of voices, everything you and I can never say about cycling not only to the world but also to our world. I've never found anything that speaks to me so clearly yet eloquently about what it means to ride, to train, to love a bike, to thrash your body and dream of greatness while understanding exactly who you are.

Now, see, there I go again. Sunsets, half price. You'll just have to read the quotes to see what I mean.

LOVE

"I took to calling my bike my friend. I carried on silent conversations with it. And of course I paid it the best attention. Which meant that everytime I returned home I stood the bike upside down, searched for a clean rag and polished the hubs and the spokes. Then I cleaned the chain and greased it afresh. That operation left ugly stains on the stone in the walkway. My mother would complain, beg me to put a newspaper under my wheel before starting to clean it. Sometimes she would get so incensed that she would say to me, in full sarcasm, 'I'm surprised you don't take that thing to bed with you!' And I would retort—'I would if I had a decent room and a big enough bed.'"

—**Henry Miller,** *My Bike and Other Friends*

Why do we love cycling?

There is no finer sport, few that are so close to the many moods of the human heart. Cycling is blur-your-eyes speed married to casual spins through sunny countryside. It is sprinting until you taste lung; it is halting on a single-track trail while silent whitetail deer cross one by one in front of you, the last one stopping and swiveling its head to look you in the eye. It is the contrast between the sleepy gathering of friends for an early-morning Sunday training ride and the Mardi Gras/Bastille Day rolling party that is the Tour de France's peloton-preceding caravan, which triples the population of every tiny French town it enters. That is why some of us love the sport.

Then there is the bicycle itself, an unparalleled merger of a toy, a utilitarian vehicle, and sporting equipment. The bicycle can be used so many ways, and approaches perfection in each use. For instance, the bicycle is the most efficient machine ever created: Converting calories into gas, a bicycle gets the equivalent of three thousand miles per gallon. A person pedaling a bike uses energy more efficiently than a gazelle or an eagle. And a triangle-frame bicycle can easily carry ten times its own weight—a capacity no automobile, airplane or bridge can match. Perfection. That is why others love the bike itself.

What's more, the bicycle is a great equalizer. The clumsiest of us, the most overweight, even people missing limbs are among those who have mastered this simple machine. Blind people ride on the back of tandems to taste the thrill of rolling along under their own power, and paraplegics scorch mountain trails on fully suspended mountain bike wheelchairs. That's why some of us love the activity.

But I think what gives our passion an edge unlike any other is its sheer versatility: the fact that cycling can be so many different things to us, sometimes even all of them at once. It's a thing with lots of splendors, as someone once said a bit more eloquently.

The quotes in this chapter are unabashed declarations or praise—some of them logical and measured, some bounding way past the limits of reason, others faint with nostalgic regret or trumpeting with hopes for no less than human redemption. In other words, pretty much what you find wherever true love exists.

"The bicycle is the noblest invention of mankind."
—**William Saroyan,** from his introduction to *The Noiseless Tenor*

"Since the bicycle makes little demand on material or energy resources, contributes little to pollution, makes a positive contribution to health and causes little death or injury, it can be regarded as the most benevolent of machines."
—**Stuart S. Wilson**

"When I see an adult on a bicycle, I do not despair for the future of the human race."
—**H. G. Wells**

"The bicycle had, and still has, a humane, almost classical moderation in the kind of pleasure it offers. It is the kind of machine that a Hellenistic Greek might have invented and ridden. It does no violence to our normal reactions: It does not pretend to free us from our normal environment."
—**J. B. Jackson**

"Think of bicycles as rideable art that can just about save the world."

—Grant Petersen

"The bicycle is the most civilized conveyance known to man. Other forms of transport grow daily more nightmarish. Only the bicycle remains pure in heart."

—Iris Murdoch, *The Red and the Green*

"When man invented the bicycle he reached the peak of his attainments. Here was a machine of precision and balance for the convenience of man. And (unlike subsequent inventions for man's convenience) the more he used it, the fitter his body became. Here, for once, was a product of man's brain that was entirely beneficial to those who used it, and of no harm or irritation to others. Progress should have stopped when man invented the bicycle."

—Elizabeth West, *Hovel in the Hills*

"How can I convey the perfection of my comfort on the bicycle, the completeness of my union with her, the sweet responses she gave me at every particle of her frame? I felt that I had known her for many years and that she had known me and that we understood each other utterly."

—**Flann O'Brien,** *The Third Policeman*

"The bicycle is its own best argument. You just get a bike, try it, start going with the thing and using it as it suits you. It'll grow and it gets better and better and better."

—**Richard Ballantine**

"When I go biking, I repeat a mantra of the day's sensations: bright sun, blue sky, warm breeze, blue jay's call, ice melting and so on. This helps me transcend the traffic, ignore the clamorings of work, leave all the mind theaters behind and focus on nature instead. I still must abide by the rules of the road, of biking, of gravity. But I am mentally far far away from civilization. The world is breaking someone else's heart."

—**Diane Ackerman**

"When the spirits are low, when the day appears dark,

when work becomes monotonous, when hope hardly seems worth having, just mount a bicycle and go out for a spin down the road, without thought on anything but the ride you are taking."

—**Arthur Conan Doyle,** in an 1896 article for
Scientific American

"After a time, habituated to spending so many hours a day on my bike, I became less and less interested in my friends. My wheel had now become my one and only friend. I could rely on it, which is more than I could say about my buddies. It's too bad no one ever photographed me with my friend. I would give anything now to know what we looked like."

—**Henry Miller,** *My Bike and Other Friends*

"As a kid I had a dream—I wanted to own my own bicycle. When I got the bike I must have been the happiest boy in Liverpool, maybe in the world. I lived for that bike. Most kids left their bikes in the backyard at night. Not me. I insisted on taking mine indoors and the first night I even kept it by my bed. Funny, although it was important to me then, I can't remember what finally happened to it."

—**John Lennon**

"Bikes are a right livelihood."
   —Scot Nicol

"Cycling is like church—many attend, but few understand."
   —Jim Burlant

"There is nothing, absolutely nothing, quite so worthwhile as simply messing about on bicycles."
   —Tom Kunich

"Dear bicycle, I shall not call you bike, you were green, like so many of your generation, I don't know why. It is a pleasure to meet it again. To describe it at length would be a pleasure. It had a little red horn instead of the bell fashionable in your days. To blow this horn was for me a real pleasure, almost a vice."
   —Samuel Beckett, *Molloy*

"On a soul whose only knowledge Was that everything was something, This was like that, that was like this— In short, everything was The bicycle of which I sing"
   —James Reaney, from *Twelve Letters to a Small Town*

"While it is a very hard and sometimes very cruel profession, my love for the bike remains as strong now as it was in the days when I first discovered it. I am convinced that long after I have stopped riding as a professional I will be riding my bicycle. I never want to abandon my bike. I see my grandfather, now in his seventies and riding around everywhere. To me that is beautiful. And the bike must always remain a part of my life."

—**Stephen Roche**

"Just as the ideal of classic Greek culture was the most perfect harmony of mind and body, so a human and a bicycle are the perfect synthesis of body and machine."

—**Richard Ballantine,** *Richards' Ultimate Bicycle Book*

"The surfer is primitive man reacting gracefully to his environment; the bicyclist is the fusion of modern man and the machine—the ultimate of man's expression with a machine he propels himself. Once one reaches motorized sport, the human becomes invisible, the cars impersonal juggernauts."

—**George Sheehan**

"Like dogs, bicycles are social catalysts that attract a superior category of people."

—**Chip Brown,** "A Bike and a Prayer"

"I took care of my wheel as one would look after a Rolls Royce. If it needed repairs I always brought it to the same shop on Myrtle Avenue run by a negro named Ed Perry. He handled the bike with kid gloves, you might say. He would always see to it that neither front nor back wheel wobbled. Often he would do a job for me without pay, because, as he put it, he never saw a man so in love with his bike as I was."

—**Henry Miller,** *My Bike and Other Friends*

"The grace and charm of the bicycle lend added warmth and contour to the persons of the lovers it joins."

—**James E. Starrs,** *The Noiseless Tenor*

"It is no longer a beast of steel . . . no . . . it is a friend. Destiny has accorded man this new friend . . . It is a faithful and powerful ally against one's worst enemies. It is stronger than anxiety, stronger than sadness. It has all the power of hope."

—**Maurice Leblanc,** *Wings to Fly*

"You can't despair for the human race when you see somebody riding a bicycle."
—**Stewart Parker**

"I love the bicycle. I always have. I can think of no sincere, decent human being, male or female, young or old, saintly or sinful, who can resist the bicycle."
—**William Saroyan,** from his introduction to *The Noiseless Tenor*

"Cycling—the sport of the century—mechanization which, together with the marvelous nature of man, triumphs over time and space."
—*La Gazzetta dello Sport*

"Nothing compares to the simple pleasure of a bike ride."
—**John F. Kennedy**

"Whoever invented the bicycle deserves the thanks of humanity."
—**Lord Charles Beresford**

MOUNTAIN BIKING

"Great things are done when men and mountains meet.
This is not done by jostling in the street."
—William Blake

Mountain Biking

The other day the crackly voice of an airline pilot announced that the plane I was sitting in would ascend to a cruising altitude of twenty-four thousand feet. Big deal, I thought, I've been half that high on my mountain bike.

That's what's cool about off-road riding: getting places you've never been, getting places most people can't. Not many people understand that. Not even some mountain bikers.

Lately, this newest incarnation of the sport has become misrepresented—appropriated by cagey marketers who correctly sensed that the raging hype of a big-air circus of speed and blood would sell more bikes. Don't get me wrong. Like most mountain bikers, I love speed. I love the still, silent moment at the top of an airborne arc when all life waits for your next move. I value hardship and become bored by a riding life without challenge, and I appreciate how a pointed rock or razored stickerbush can remind us that we are soft things on a solid earth. I even like that mountain biking can sometimes be a stupid thing in a sensible society, I admire bike acrobatics, and when I watch the face of pro downhillers preparing for a run I vow to find more of their bravado in my own soul. I have the scars and stories of brash idiocy to prove all of this.

But mountain biking is more. Mountain biking is more

than blurry images on fast-paced commercials selling soft drinks or sport-recreation vehicles. At its best, mountain biking is even bigger than the mountain. You can just be out somewhere, alone or with a few friends who know how to be alone together, and find yourself in a kind of isolated beauty of your own creation that's all the more wonderful because it is happening in our world of instant information delivery and constant information assaults.

I've found moments like this at ten thousand feet in Crested Butte, Colorado, when I inadvertently rode off the front of a small group then stopped to sip some water and wait for them, turning as I leaned against my bike until I faced a cathedral of bare rock that stretched beyond clouds, beyond comprehension or imagination. I know this didn't happen but I would still swear that for a single instant every bird and insect fell silent, and I could no longer hear my friends romping up the trail, and the mountain took a step toward me.

I've also found mountain biking moments at four hundred feet in Pennsylvania foothills, when one Thanksgiving my trail dog Lucy flushed eight turkey over my head in an organic fireworks show of feathers and swirling leaves that unlike other memories is never less distinct when I recall it.

You can't sell that brand of mountain biking to the public, though—at least not in a thirty-second television spot or a two-page magazine ad—and that's probably a tragedy.

"The spirit of mountain biking is cool. I hope racing never dominates it."
   —Susan DeMattei

"Mountain biking can't be square and clean-cut 'cause it's not a square sport. It's gotta stay tribal."
   —Missy Giove

"There's this downhill jump at Lake Isabella, near my parents' house, that I absolutely love. It defines everything I like about the sport. You get 40 feet of air. You launch off this drop-off, and you're airborne. One of the best things about it is that you don't know where you're going to land. It took me a long time to get my huevos together to actually do it. When you're in the air, your mind completely empties, and you're just doing it."
   —Dave Cullinan

"I don't ride for the money so much, or for the fame. I ride for my heart. I'm a soul rider."

—Steve Cook

"Here's the big question. Before you answer it, close your eyes. Hit the dirt. Stuff is flying. You are flying. Speeding. Finessing singletracks. Lifting over rocks. Everything is flying. Try it again. Feel the earth. Hear your breathing. Go slow. Climb the mountain. See that deer. Make eye contact. Stop. Now, the question: Why does it matter? What's special? Why is being a helmet-headed, Lycra-wearing, suspension-luv'n, rock-stomping, off-road pin-up wannabe such a cool thing?"

—Dan Koeppel

"You're moving through a wonderful natural environment and working on balance, timing, depth perception, judgment . . . It forms kind of a ballet."

—Charlie Cunningham

"Mountain biking offers recreation, freedom, transportation, sport and the opportunity to get far away from it all."
   —Charlie Kelly

"It's a feeling you get on certain trails, when you're reacting like you and your machine are just one thing. It's the feel of physical exertion and speed and technique all wrapped into one."
   —Ned Overend

"I'm lucky that mountain biking wasn't around when I was 20, because I wouldn't have won the Tour de France. It's my kind of sport—hard, individualistic, and not a lot of tactics."
   —Greg LeMond

"Mountain biking is like a drug for me. I do it because I enjoy it."
   —Rudy de Bie

"I know myself through mountain biking. That's how I center myself if things are out of whack personally."
   —Myles Rockwell

"It's freeing, the sense of detached awareness found only on the best mountain bike rides. I'm no longer me. I'm a rolling ball of intent. Ride over that rock. Go wide on the curve. It's hard but there's no place I'd rather be. There's no place but here. No time but now."
—Don Cuerdon

"I've seen mountain bike rides transform people—not just their bodies but their way of thinking. Their spirit."
—Charlie Cunningham

"As a pack undulates along a trail, it forms an organism. Because energy concentrates at the head, the amount of juice you receive depends on whether you're blasting off the front, hanging mid-pack, or re-experiencing your lunch way off the back."
—Lee McCormack

"Hardship is relative. That's the beauty of it. A rider chugging up a hill for the first time might see her struggle as a near-fatal triumph. A more-seasoned rider might find her heart of darkness in a month-long trek across dangerous, untouched terrain. What's wonderful about mountain biking is that these two riders might be the same person separated by just a few months experience."

—Dan Koeppel

"Really good mountain bikers are lousy judges of trail difficulty. We haven't a clue, we just ride."

—John Olsen

"I was a Category 1 road racer, maybe one of the top fifty riders in the country, and nobody in town gave a hoot. But I was a local hero for beating that guy over the hill, Joe Breeze, in the Repack."

—Gary Fisher

"We were just having fun. I always liked that line. It's true—that's all we were doing in the late '70s. People think there was some marketing genius behind the development of mountain bikes, but we were just having fun."

—Joe Breeze

"In 1974, I blacksmithed the now famous klunker from scavenged objects. Then I started to hear that high form of recognition: 'You can't do that,' and, 'It won't work.' I knew I was onto something big."
　　—Gary Fisher

"There were many steps in the evolution of the mountain bike. There was no single inventor."
　　—Joe Breeze

"When mountain biking was a tiny, tiny sport I had a big part in it. Now that it's a big, big sport I have a tiny part in it."
　　—Victor Vincente of America

"From the age of four, when I got my first bike, riding was the main focus for me. Almost every day I was on the thing, and I just loved riding. It becomes a part of your body, and all the movements just become one hundred percent natural. When you get to that point on a mountain bike, then you're a good rider."
　　—John Tomac

"I'm trying my hardest to practice 'no brakes, no brains.' That doesn't mean I'm not thinking, being careful, responsible, or safe. It means that I'm letting my instincts guide me away from the world of cautious fears and toward the pleasure that resides out there on the edge."

—Dan Koeppel

"The thing about picking a good line is that you're already feeling great about just being on a bike, just rolling along, and then something starts to feel special, something you can't put your finger on, but you just realize that you're not overbraking, not oversteering, that the tires are carving like skates, that you come out of corners with momentum, and that it almost feels like the trail is controlling the bike and you're just along for the ride. I haven't a clue how to achieve it, or repeat it, except in some Zenlike way of not trying, but I know that I live for that: the perfect line."

—Steve Casimiro

"Our paths to off-road mastery reflect our personalities. Analyzers study every element. Finessers search for the line of least resistance. Muscle barons assume sheer power will overcome all obstacles. Then there are the freelancers. They hop on any bike and go. They're superb riders and their learning process is purely visceral. They're masters of instant choreography—doing whatever's necessary to keep going."

—Hank Barlow

"I imagine that I'm a cat, ready to land anywhere."

—Paul Willerton

"You know right away in mountain biking if you're on or not."

—Alison Sydor

"If you feel bad in a road race and you get dropped, usually there's a group you can ride in with. You can joke around with everybody else who got dropped, and trade snacks or whatever. But in a mountain bike race there's nowhere to hide."

—John Tomac

"Off the back, you get psychic help from no one. When you're close, you can tap into the collective might. Borrow some energy, increase your speed (thereby increasing your thrill) and catch up. But when you're way OTB, forget it. If you want to cruise, fine. Otherwise, it's just you, your pain, and your lunch, for the second time."
—**Lee McCormack**

DON'T TRUST ANYONE UNDER 5,000 FEET.
—**T-shirt** at 1991 national championship race in
Mammoth, California

"Messengers and mountain bikers share a common chromosome."
—**James Bethea**

"Riding in snow is like learning to ski. There's a definite learning curve, and an appreciation of freaked-out recoveries that comes with time. Sooner or later, you'll gain a whole new admiration for funky moves."
—**Tom Winter**

"Snow riding is a little crazy and, thus, good for the spirit. Your tires produce a musical crunch and artistic tread patterns. Anyone who says that mountain bikers are always occupied with speed and precision doesn't have a clue."
—Tim Blumenthal

"Riding trails with your dog restores a bond lost in some evolutionary belch. You travel at the same speed, over the same terrain, neither of you slowing to compensate for the other. You're equal playmates with mud in your teeth."
—Allison Glock

"If it ain't moto, it's worthless."
—Ross Shafer

"One natural earthquake does more damage than ten thousand unnatural trail bikers, and still the mountain stands."
—Jon Carroll

"Mountain biking helps people become environmentalists. A mountain bike is a vehicle to appreciate the backcountry."
—Ned Overend

"Ultimately, soft cycling is a way of life, a way of thinking that stretches well beyond mountain biking. It's an awareness that the world and ourselves are constantly evolving, and that what we may arrogantly call right in our youth may be seen as humorous or destructive in our maturing. Who knows what mountain bikes will look like and be capable of in the future? Maybe those who fear our fat tires will be proven right, or maybe a new age of environmentalism will cite the mountain bike as our salvation."
   —Hank Barlow

"Shred lightly."
   —Scot Nicol

"When you're dressed like an alien from planet Neon, to a hiker you look like you're ten miles per hour faster than you are. In a quiet, forested area, for someone to come around a bend at even twelve mph dressed like this looks out of place and it can be really offensive."
   —Hank Barlow

"I know I should be upset because outlaw trail cyclists are cutting new trails through the Mount Tamalpais watershed. But actually, I'm not. Cyclists are said to present sundry dangers both to the land and to the spiritually evolved hikers. I think perhaps their main crime is that they are having too much fun. Nature, as we know, is a cathedral and a temple and for Godsakes keep your voice down and show some respect."
—Jon Carroll

"They [Shimano's Japan headquarters] give me a test bike that weighs like sixty pounds—a total tank—plus a backpack. It's all wired so they can measure all sorts of things. And they give you a little microphone for your comments. So I take off down their test track, and I'm hooting and hollering, like 'gnarly!' Or, 'shredding!' Or, 'roosted their mug!' A couple days later they play back the tape and say, 'Ah you make some comments here. We are not sure what you mean.' "
—Greg Herbold

"Until mountain biking came along, the bike scene was ruled by a small elite cadre of people who seemed allergic to enthusiasm."
—Jacquie Phelan

"Thanks to the mountain bike revolution, you no longer need to be a roadie to be an elitist."
— **Don Cuerdon**

"Mountain biking's cult status died the day Madonna started riding."
— *Bike* **magazine**

"I think mountain biking has grown up; it's an adult now. As a kid, you have nothing but fun. As an adult, you have pressure, you have to pay the bills."
— **Dale Hughes**

"The simple sport of mountain biking doesn't really exist anymore. The simple Sunday ride will never change, but the racing already has and will continue to."
— **Alison Sydor**

"There's something wrong. We're losing ground. I don't hear people talking about fun and enjoyment. I hear radical, gnarly, fast, suspended, Lycra, titanium. I don't hear sensing, the environment, and feeling."
— **Bob Seals**

"It's funny. Die-hard dirtheads believe that everyone should get a mountain bike, yet they bum out over the fact that just about anyone can. Because if everyone has one, how do you tell who the true mountain bikers are?"
—**Rob Story**

"All mountain bikers are not created equal. And that's fine. I don't know why so many people seem so eager to stuff this great activity into some phony homogeneous straitjacket, as if we're all alike—young, speed-crazed gonzos living life with the same identity. It just ain't true. Some ride for nature. Some for thrill. Others for fitness. There are riders who hate uphills and would rather take a car. Some riders hate cars. Some riders smoke cigarettes as they ride. Some actually look like they inhabit a Mountain Dew commercial. Some hate suspension. Some live for it. Some love riding road bikes. Some don't. Whatever."
—**Zapata Espinoza**

"Ignaz was a stud. If Ignaz were alive today, he'd think mountain bikes were bitchin'."
—**Greg Bagni,** on the founder of Schwinn

ROAD RIDING

"To sweep down hills and plunge into valley hollows; to cover as on wings the far stretches of the road ahead and to find them in bloom at your approach."
—**Alain Fournier,** *The Wanderer*

These days I ride with the body and brain of a mountain biker, but with the soul of a roadie. I think I'm happy about this—even though a pure mountain bike pedigree would let me levitate over rockfields, add five seconds of hangtime to my jumps, and cause my goatee to grow in gnarlier.

But there's not much I can do about who I am. I became what some people call a "serious" cyclist just after Merckx, during the glory of Hinault and the beginning of LeMond, when Campy Super Record was a totem of titans. Racing bikes really were "ten-speeds." Shifting was an un-indexed art that happened from the down tube instead of the handlebar, and clips-and-straps were the only pedals there were.

It's not that I think those days were somehow better or purer. I love modern technology: clipless pedals, brake/shift levers, sixteen (and beyond) gear choices, the suppleness of titanium, lightness of oversized aluminum and composite mixes, and the lively feel of computer-butted steel that can't be found on any other kind of frame. And let there be no doubt: Armstrong and Museeuw would be hardguys in any era, Virenque and Pantani could outclimb the peloton of any past decade.

All I'm saying is that, like anyone, I am who life made me. Road riding was my first love. The road was freedom and speed. It found my weaknesses and hammered them into strengths. I learned meditation on long solo sessions, strategy in packs, and ruthlessness in sprints. My pulse attuned itself to the rhythm of road riding, and my heart beats that way still. Too long on dirt and I begin to crave humming along three-up with good friends. I savor the casual warm-up, the way someone is always getting feisty and going off the front after promising an easy ride, the things you say to each other that you seem to only be capable of saying while the pedals are spinning. I need to find a paceline crackling with adrenaline, a descent to carve, a smooth ribbon of pavement that curls away to the horizon, and a trusted wheel to follow.

"I was not yet sixteen when I understood a great deal, from having ridden bicycles for so long, about style, speed, grace, purpose, value, form, integrity, health, humor, music, breathing, and finally and perhaps best of all the relationship between the beginning and the end."

—**William Saroyan,** *The Bicycle Rider in Beverly Hills*

"All creatures who have ever walked have wished that they might fly. With highwheelers a flesh and blood man can hitch wings to his feet."

—**Karl Kron,** *Ten Thousand Miles on a Bicycle*

"It is all very well to say to yourself that you are not thinking as you wheel serenely along; but you are, and that sure uncertainty of the cyclist's balance, that unconsciously watchful suspension (solid on earth yet so breezily flitting) seems to symbolize the task itself."

—**Christopher Morley,** *The Romany Stain*

"If you ride you know those moments when you have fed yourself into the traffic, felt the hashed-up asphalt rattle in the handlebars, held a lungful of air in a cloud of exhaust. Up ahead there are two parallel buses. With cat's whiskers, you measure the clearance down a doubtful alley. You swing wide, outflank that flower truck. The cross-street yellow light is turning red. You burst off the green like a surfer on a wave of metal. You have a hundred empty yards of Broadway to yourself."

—**Chip Brown,** "A Bike and a Prayer"

"Most bicyclists in New York City obey instinct far more than they obey the traffic laws, which is to say that they run red lights, go the wrong way on one-way streets, violate cross-walks, and terrify innocents, because it just seems easier that way. Cycling in the city, and particularly in midtown, is anarchy without malice."

—*New Yorker* "Talk of the Town" section

"What I loved about bike racing was that it was not a mainstream sport. My heroes were self-made. There were no coaches, no training centers, and only a handful of sponsors. Training rides were not totally devoted to bike talk. I got to know a lot of riders this way, not just as good sprinters or good climbers, but as people who had ideas different from mine, jobs different from mine, and dreams different from mine. I prefer that world of bike riding and racing to the present one."

—**Steve Tesich**

"The turn of the century was a splendid time for the bicycle. It was an industry, a sport, a vehicle for transport."
—**Dick Swann**

"I mean, you either love spinning the pedals and watching scenery whiz by, or you don't. And if you love it, not much can sour you on the idea of riding your bike."
—**Keith Mills**

"The bicycle gives you individualism which is not only rugged but smooth and purring underneath, as witness the sound of rubber tires on damp streets."
—**Henry Beetle Hough,** *Singing in the Morning*

"The bicycle ran with special ease at dusk, the tire emitting a kind of whisper as it palpated each rise and dip in the hard earth along the edge of the road."
—**Vladimir Nabokov,** *Mary*

"Sometimes the road was only a lane, with thick hawthorn hedges, and the green elms overhung it on either side so that when you looked up there was only a strip of blue sky

between. And as you rode along in the warm, keen air you had a sensation that the world was standing still and life would last forever. Although you were pedaling with such energy you had a delicious feeling of laziness."
—**W. Somerset Maugham,** *Cakes and Ale*

"You never have the wind with you—either it is against you or you're having a good day."
—**Daniel Behrman,** *The Man Who Loved Bicycles*

"If the wind is not against you, it is not blowing."
—**James E. Starrs,** *The Noiseless Tenor*

"The century. A cheap analogy for life. Little pains happen. You adjust. A lot of it is dull stuff indeed, but you make the effort. Man and machine become one organism, stroking away, correcting, favoring, compensating, and trying to enjoy the little moments of magic that come along. At the end of it, you get off the bike, or fall off, or are pushed off, and that is it."
—**John D. MacDonald,** *Condominium*

"There is always unpleasantness about this tandem. It is the theory of the man in front that the man behind does nothing; it is equally the theory of the man behind that he alone is the motive power, the man in front merely doing the puffing. The mystery will never be solved."

—**Jerome K. Jerome,** *Three Men on the Bummel*

"Suddenly he'd wake up and notice that he was pedaling very slowly, as though his legs were hesitating, pondering. Only when he'd concentrate all his attention on the relationship of body and bicycle (the sensation of motion) and speed up his pedaling, carefully breathing, until he'd experience a bearable and pleasant feeling of exertion, would his contentment be complete. He'd feel in tune with himself. Rushing downhill, sometimes with the wind coming from a certain angle, this feeling would soar very high."

—**Uwe Johnson,** *The Third Book About Achim*

"Picture its bare-bones beauty. The delicate balance of power and elegance you use to make it fly. The tires singing on pavement, chain purring on the sprockets, the seamless paceline hurtling you and your friends home at 25 mph. Beats there a heart so hard that it can't

love a road bike?"
—**Scott Martin**

"I wonder if the decline in road bike sales isn't also a reaction to the perfection of the road bike. Maybe once you get everything you want, you lose interest. Back when road bikes had cottered cranks, Simplex derailleurs made of flimsy plastic, Universal brakes that couldn't arrest the forward motion of a determined box turtle, and tires so miserable they will remain nameless (Hutchinson; I lied), you could hardly wait to buy a better one. Now, with factories pumping out an endless stream of perfect bicycles— functionally perfect anyway—who cares?"
—**Ted Costantino**

"Smooth, predictable riding when you're in a group isn't just a matter of style. It's survival."
—**Geoff Drake**

"A good rider is intuitive. You can look at other cyclists and know just how good they are by how they pedal or breathe."
—**Thurlow Rogers**

"The pack is a single, fickle entity, a blaze of color leaving only a trail of dust in its vacuum wake. Even the most pervasive social conventions fall by the wayside under physical stress, as mere survival takes precedence over winning. The pack may be heedless of its own stragglers and have no more sympathy or sense of smell than hounds chasing a fox. In the end, you are on your own, a particle in the false constant of motion."
   —Laurence Malone

"There are a lot of people with expectations that U. S. cycling will become a big sport like it is in Europe. But you have to be realistic. I don't care what American football does, it isn't going to be as big in Europe as it is in the U. S. People grow up with a sport—that's what makes it big. That's what has to happen with cycling in the U.S."
   —Greg LeMond

"A road rider who is unpracticed is merely an athlete on a bike, half-educated, a pedaler—not a complete cyclist."
   —Maynard Hershon

"A road racer without endurance is like a bicycle without wheels."

—**James E. Starrs,** *The Noiseless Tenor*

"You not bike rider, you nobody."

—**Eddie B**

CLIMBING

"The bikers rode past. They were moving so fast. Hills were nothing to them. They had light bikes, expensive ones, and the climbs were only excuses to use the great strength of their legs."

—**Rick Bass,** *The Watch*

CLIMBING

Climbing is the forge. It hardens you or it breaks you, and you usually won't know which until you feel the fire.

I acknowledge this with a sort of mad joy because if the cycling gods blessed me at all it was with a climbing gene. This does not mean I am a great ascender. It just means I am less inept at it than I am at the rest of cycling. That is, relative only to myself, I am a polka-dot jersey winner but out among the big boys I am happy just to hang. If I'm having a good day and a good rider is suffering a bad day, I might even be able to throw a little hurt on him. A tiny little hurt.

Before I knew much about cycling, my opinion of my ability used to be a little bigger—like, say, bigger than a hors categorie climb. Two events changed that. One was a climbing camp I attended: seven days on Virginia's Blue Ridge mountains, following instructors Betsy King (who among her 400 victories can count the climber's jersey in the women's Tour de France) and Anna Schwartz (who twice set the women's solo 24-hour record). On a training ride about midweek the group dropped me like I was something that had fallen off a tall building. As I craned my neck to watch the pack scale another asphalt wall in the middle of farms and nothing else, my delirium seemingly peaked and I began hearing music—a blues harmonica providing a soundtrack for my fatigue. Then I spotted a Category 1 road racer from Chicago named Mike Zaug sitting up amid the speeding pack, hands off the bar, playing a harmonica to pass the time. Now there's a climber.

A few years later I talked my way into a commissar's car at the Tour DuPont, America's biggest stage race. A com car is like a police car that patrols the race to make sure the riders don't do illegal things. Our job for this time trial stage was to make sure racers didn't cut the course or accept drafts from the team cars that shadowed them to supply a spare wheel or mechanical help in an emergency. Just before the biggest climb, we dropped behind Thierry Claveyrolat, a lean French pro who'd won the King of the Mountain jersey twice in the Dauphine Libere and once in the Tour de France.

The road bent skyward and our automatic transmission dropped down a gear. Claveyrolat popped out of the saddle, dipped his bike from side to side in an elegant dance, then sat back down and spun out his pedals.

"Twenty-two," announced the European driver. "Not bad." Not at all, I figured. Twenty-two kilometers must be something like thirteen or fourteen miles per hour on this hellish ascent. Then the driver said,

"Twenty-four . . . no, twenty-five miles an hour."

Thierry Claveyrolat, I bow to you.

"It's really something to see, a climber waiting to attack. Any other sort of attack can be neutralized, but when a climber goes there's little the non-climbers can do."
   —**Ralph Hurne,** *The Yellow Jersey*

"One by one each man ran out of energy and collapsed under Bartali's relentless pressure. He became once again the dazzling magician of the summits, flying on the mountains, reducing to nothing all those who, moments before, were his adversaries. On this execrable planet his gracious pedaling couldn't help but exhort admiration."
   —**Jacques Goddett**

"It would be dangerous to follow Ottavio Bottecchia up a mountain pass. It would be suicidal. His progression is so powerful and regular that we would end up asphyxiated."
   —**Nicolas Frantz**

"We both attacked the climb at the same time. I gave it everything. I looked up and, unbelievably, he was at least twenty paces in front of me. He was moving so gracefully, like a bird, floating past people—or perhaps more a gliding process. There is nobody in the peloton who can ride like that. Absolutely nobody."

—**Paul Kimmage,** on Stephen Roche

"Henri Pelissier's climbing ranks as art. He climbs using the full range of his abilities, from the force of his legs to the acumen of his mind and surety of his judgment. Pelissier knows how to play his instrument."

—**Henri Desgrange**

"You can say that climbers suffer the same as the other riders, but they suffer in a different way. You feel the pain, but you're glad to be there."

—**Richard Virenque**

"Perhaps the best reason to enjoy hill climbing is that it has something all great sports possess: the marriage of brute strength and finely honed technique."

—**Steve Casimiro**

"I used to be able to climb up one mountain, any mountain, faster than anybody. When I had to begin training my body to hold up over however many mountains might come, I lost that raw speed. I had a stronger motor, but I didn't have a big punch."
—Andy Hampsten

"You want to be like a carpet unrolling. Get faster as the climb goes on."
—Chris Carmichael

"If you blow at the bottom, you're gone. Better to ride within yourself and start picking people off. This doesn't mean giving up, because sometimes the speed is really high at the bottom and then it mellows. But you have to realize what your capabilities are. It's always better to blow later than earlier."
—Mike Engleman

"Don't buy upgrades, ride up grades."
—Anonymous

"If you need a push in the mountains, looking really sick or completely knackered is a sure-fire way of getting crowd sympathy. However, should a commissar spot you getting a push, shout loudly and at least your fine that night won't be for a solicited push."

—Robert Millar

"You don't want to be in the lowest gear too often. Really steep climbs are not my forte, so I always dread that lowest gear because I figure, god, I'm doomed."

—Juli Furtado

"Just go steady and hard up all the hills. People don't mind riding fast and slow, fast and slow, but they hate a hard, steady pace."

—Heidi Hopkins

"A lot of times you're told to keep your upper body as still as possible. But when I climb, I don't follow this rule. If you're sitting perfectly still, you're stiff. You shouldn't move too much, but some upper-body movement is necessary if you're to find a rhythm."

—Atle Kvalsvoll

"The commercials have made it so that we forget that a lot of mountain biking is grunting up climbs, and being rewarded with that maybe ten percent of the time when you're breezing down the other side."
—Jacquie Phelan

"Beyond the challenge, the head games, the learning, the fitness factor, the aesthetics and the technical problems, there's one major reason to climb hills. It begins with a D."
—Steve Casimiro

"What is it that makes climbers? How is it that two of the best racers, together at the foot of a mountain, can be divided by ten or more minutes at the summit? Genetics? Suppleness? Lightness? Attitude? Training? There is no one quality which makes the difference."
—David Walsh, *Inside the Tour de France*

"Every year I can't wait to get to the mountains. I'm really impatient. . . The real mountains are what I like, where the roads are black with people, where they just move apart enough to let you through. It makes your spine tingle. When you are racing like that those moments are incredibly emotive. You think about them for the rest of the year."

—Richard Virenque

"The climbs have been awesome. When I was young, seeing the pictures of the Vuelta in *VeloNews,* I always thought, 'God, that would be incredible.' And now I've been there . . . it gives me goosebumps."

—Bobby Julich, after riding his first Tour of Spain

"People are screaming and the next thing you know you're going too hard. You're out of the saddle sprinting up a hill or something and because of the cheers you don't feel a thing until you get to the top. Then you pay."

—Alison Sydor

"I had been familiar with that street for years, and had supposed it was dead level: But it was not, as the bicycle now informed me to my surprise. The bicycle, in the hands of a novice, is as alert and acute as a spirit-level in the detecting and vanishing shades of difference in these matters. It notices a rise where your untrained eye would not observe that one existed."

—Mark Twain, "Taming the Bicycle"

"If you never confront climbs, you're missing the essence of the sport. With ascents come adversity. Without adversity there's no challenge. Without challenge, no improvement, no sense of accomplishment, no deep-down joy."

—Betsy King

"The people in Italy still talk about it. It reminds them of the old glory years when it wasn't just one rider against another, but racing out on the open roads, where anything can happen and where a guy who perseveres can come out on top. There was a lot of hard luck going around that day, and it reminded people of the great things in bike racing."

—Andy Hampsten, on his epic 1988 ride over Gavia
Pass through snow and ice to win the Giro d'Italia

"Getting up at six and racing up a col from the gun is a bitch."

—Jacky Durand

DESCENDING

"He dropped down the hills on his bicycle. The roads were greasy, so he had to let it go. He felt a pleasure as the machine plunged over the second, steeper drop in the hill. . . . His bicycle seemed to fall beneath him, and he loved it."

—D. H. Lawrence, *Sons and Lovers*

On the road, descending has always been a hallowed ability; a good descender gets a kind of respect unlike that given even to the greatest champions—an acknowledgment that in this rare person daring and skill appear in equal measure. Disproportionate amounts send you skidding across asphalt or off cliffs or, worst of all, turn you into a brake dragger.

But if the gift is hallowed, it is also a bit hollowed. A pro such as Sean Yates can surpass sixty mph on the steepest and longest descents, dropping a pack or regaining minutes from a break as he lays his bike flat out through hairpins and throws it sideways across twisted roads. Even so, great downhillers never win races because of their specialty the way great sprinters do. And they never shatter a field or demoralize leaders the way a climber or straight-ahead power rider can.

It was with mountain biking that descending became a thing of victory and, perhaps someday, legend. Enveloped in post-apocalyptic body armor exoskeletons, mountain bike downhillers hurtle over surfaces that couldn't safely be walked. At fifty or fifty-five mph, choking and blinded from dust, they will their bikes to bite through shifty rocks and loose dirt to find the hard bone of a mountain. They leap as high as a roof, soaring thirty feet off a good launch. Then they laugh about it and go up for another run, embracing what most of us try all our lives to avoid.

They share something with the great road descenders, though—and with you and me for that matter. The great and strange downhiller Missy Giove calls it "flow." It's a sensation felt only during a brilliant descent, sometimes for the length of the run, sometimes for only a few minutes. Or a few feet. But it is there, and the few times I have fallen into it I was reminded afterward exactly of Missy's description. Flow is something like what a fish must feel, the fastest fish swimming with a current, completely in your element yet caught by something unresistable and as strong as the earth itself.

I flowed for twenty-five glorious minutes once, from the crest of one of Washington's Cascade mountains to its midpoint. A trail-care crew had groomed a singletrack just hours before. Twisty quick tight turns banked so you never touch your brakes across a meadow of wheel-high wildflowers and grass that falls down, down, down, down and down. Punching gears and carving. Surfing. Floating. Flying. Out of my mind, then out of my body. Twenty-five of the greatest minutes of my life, when I knew exactly what it was to be alive but did not have to think about it at all.

"The difference between the best and the rest in down-hilling cannot be attributed to just one thing. You must stay as composed as possible. If you think you are going to fall, it will happen. You must anticipate the maximum speed you can use on every part of the course—and good technique is essential."
   —Francois Gachet

"It's not the fastest rider who wins a downhill, it's the one who gets to the bottom in the shortest time."
   —Greg Herbold

"Downhill is not a big-air event. It's a speed event. The closer you stay to the ground, the faster you go. When you lose contact with the ground you lose momentum. It's gospel for downhillers."
   —Myles Rockwell

"When I'm godawful close to the edge—a cliff, a tree—I try to get through it by believing in myself and saying, 'I can pull this off,' rather than hitting the brake."
—Missy Giove

"On scary sections, you need to make your body and mind agree with each other. Both have to say, 'Let's go there.'"
—Franck Roman

"I almost always hit my maximum heart rate in the downhill. It's like a pursuit race on the track. The downhill's a short, one hundred percent sprint with one hundred percent concentration."
—John Tomac

"I've worked on my downhilling, and I've gotten a lot smoother. Go smoother and you go fast."
—Tinker Juarez

"I only descend fast in races, not in training. And my descending in racing is totally instinctual. I'm only thinking of someone ahead of me or behind me."

—**Juli Furtado**

"I've never really trained for downhill, except at the races. I have done eleven seasons cross-country and I want to focus on downhill before I retire. I'm pretty big and it's not easy to pull my big skeleton uphill."

—**John Tomac**

"Attaining a flow state—that's your goal when descending. I hit it every ride, sometimes for the whole ride, sometimes just for part. Let it come and take you."

—**Missy Giove**

"I usually descend better when I'm in second place. When I'm trying to catch somebody, I go down cleaner than if I'm trying to hold a lead."

—**Juli Furtado**

"If you're on rocks or an unstable surface, you've got to let go of the brakes until you get to a place where you can apply them. This means that sometimes you have to go faster than you'd like. Letting go of the brakes in order to get back on a good line is one of the hardest technical things to learn."

—**John Tomac**

"The best way to ride, especially downhill, is with both hands in your pockets and leaning backwards. This is not so hard as it looks; like a bird, you control your direction perfectly by unconscious shifts in your balance. Especially on the long downslopes, this is to know the freedom of the wind."

—**Louis J. Halle, Jr.,** *Spring in Washington*

"I'm worried that when I descend I won't have the same fearlessness, that I will be afraid of hurting myself. You can't afford to be afraid of riding in the group, or of fear itself. One day recently I tried descending flat-out, and without thinking about it I was flying and taking risks. I felt liberated."

—**Marco Pantani,** on his recovery from a head-on collision with a car

"I think when you're on the edge of life like a downhill racer is, you have to be spiritual. For me, it'd be odd not to think about death and spirituality."

—**Missy Giove**

"There's no athletic ability needed to descend, just an iron nerve and the ability to really control a bike . . . It's a useful asset in mountain racing, because often a man who can't climb too well is able, on the descent, to catch the climbers who dropped him on the way up. Often minutes can be gained without turning a pedal, just by sitting on your machine and leaving more nervous riders behind. And there's something to be nervous about. You can drop like a stone on unsurfaced roads with hairpin bends where a slight miscalculation can mean possible death and certain injury. A descending cyclist can reach speeds of sixty-five miles per hour, and at this speed brakes are useless and a puncture disastrous. Riders have been killed or maimed through descending accidents. The mountain roads are unfenced and often a sheer drop waits for a rider who miscalculates."

—**Ralph Hurne,** *The Yellow Jersey*

"I like fear. I like knowing that if I make a mistake, whether it's all over or not is in my hands."
—Jake Watson

"My favorite courses are nasty, technical downhills that frighten my mom."
—Josh Ivey

"I've never been on a course that intimidated me."
—Mike King

"When in doubt, gas it!"
—Greg Herbold

"You don't get scared. You don't have time to be."
—John Tomac, on Mammoth Mountain's Kamikaze downhill race

"Downhill's the future of the sport. Cross-country's not geared for TV. Some fat guy watching it with a beer in one hand and potato chips in the other is going to say, 'I can do that.' America likes to see people crash."
—**Missy Giove**

"Showing crashes all the time makes a joke of the sport and makes it look crazy. This has nothing to do with what the sport is really about. It is so difficult to manage the bike and yourself on a downhill course. This does not come across."
—**Francois Gachet**

"Downhilling is the proving ground for bikes. You never subject a bike to so brutal a torture in cross-country. Downhillers have speed in them that's beyond the bike."
—**Steve Gravenites**

"Downhillers do have an image of being crazy. But if we were really crazy, we wouldn't last long. I like to call it professional craziness."
—**Greg Herbold**

"Are downhillers crazy? Sure. They've got to have a wild streak to be successful. Stupidity isn't what I mean. They've got to force the survival instinct out of their minds. I have a ton of respect for them."

—Ned Overend

"If you can't beat them up the hill, you have to find a way to beat them on the way down."

—Steve Hegg, explaining his ten-tooth cog

"They could die out there. I've seen broken frames, bent cranks, disintegrated pedals, crumpled disk wheels, suspension forks that broke in half."

—Steve Gravenites, on mountain bike downhill racers

SPEED, SPRINTING, AND THE NOISELESS RUSH

"I came out for exercise, gentle exercise, and to notice the scenery and to botanise. And no sooner do I get on that accursed machine than off I go hammer and tongs; I never look to right or left, never notice a flower, never see a view—get hot, juicy, red—like a grilled chop. Get me on that machine and I have to go. I go scorching along the road, and cursing aloud at myself for doing it."

—H.G. Wells, *The Wheels of Chance*

You notice the burn high in your thigh first—a small, tiny burn more like a single nerve tingling, or as if some weightless insect had landed there then flitted off. It is just the smallest sensation, really, so you spin out your cadence. You click out one more gear and still the whirling of your legs is effortless. You go. You go. Some small thing carried by the wind pings off your cheek and when you feel that suddenly your legs wake up from a nightmare and begin screaming.

But you go. You curl into the bike and grab a handful of gears, and your breath fogs the shiny exposed metal of the handlebar and you go. You go. You gulp a mouthful of air that stretches the corners of your lips and stings the back of your throat and then you jump, you stand above the bike and put it all into the pedals and the frame flexes beneath you and your chest feels unzipped, and the chain wails and a high-pitched noise that does not exist stuns your ears. And you go. You go.

Real people do not understand speed the same way we do. They know it only from the seat of a car, so they have no idea of the force and finesse required to propel a person on a bicycle at twenty miles per hour, let alone twenty-five, thirty, thirty-five—or the inhumane forty-plus hit by the great sprinters and trackies. Real people might remember from a physics class that wind resistance increases exponentially rather than linearly with speed, but they have never been taught this by having the wind punch them in the face then swirl down their bodies and settle around their legs like concrete. Their loss.

Because only we know the noiseless rush and the curious smoothing of the roughest trail or road that comes with enough momentum. Only we understand the satisfaction of driving yourself—instead of being driven—faster than we were meant to go. And only we get the urge to do it again, but faster this time.

In 1899, pacing himself behind a steam locomotive, a man named Charles Murphy rode his bicycle one mile in 57 4/5 seconds along planks laid between the tracks, breaking the mile-a-minute barrier before an automobile had. In 1985, John Howard rode 152.284 mph behind a pace car on Utah's Bonneville Salt Flats, and then ten years later on the same surface a cyclist named Fred Rompelberg bettered him by going 166.9 mph behind a pace car. That same year, Christian Taillefer rode an unpaced mountain bike 111 miles per hour down a ski slope in Vars, France. You go.

"Tens of thousands who could never afford to own, feed and stable a horse, had by this bright invention enjoyed the swiftness of motion which is perhaps the most fascinating feature of material life."

—**Frances Willard,** *How I Learned to Ride the Bicycle*

"Bicycling is the nearest approximation I know to the flight of birds. The airplane simply carries a man on its back like an obedient Pegasus; it gives him no wings of his own."

—**Louis J. Halle, Jr.,** *Spring in Washington*

"If you desire to be groovy and flowing instead of battling and conquering, miles-per-hour is the last equation you want to pay attention to."

—**Bob Roll**

"Next to a leisurely walk I enjoy a spin on my tandem bicycle. It is splendid to feel the wind blowing in my face and the springy motion of my iron steed. The rapid rush through the air gives me a delicious sense of strength and buoyancy, and the exercise makes my pulse dance and my heart sing."

—**Helen Keller,** *The Story of My Life*

"I like riding track bikes, especially once you get up to speed because it's so easy to stay at that speed. At 10 or 15 miles an hour it's like coasting all the time."
　—Sukeun Chun

"I actually feel it's my obligation to go fast."
　—Myles Rockwell

"It's me who is pedaling."
　—Bernard Hinault, replying to fans telling him he
　　can go faster

"It was a fact I've always wanted a bike. Speed gave me a thrill."
　—Alan Sillitoe, "The Bike"

"There is something uncanny in the noiseless rush of the cyclist, as he comes into view, passes by, and disappears."
　—*Popular Science*, 1891

"Sometimes, when she rode hard, when she could really proj, Chevette got free of everything: the city, her body, even time. That was the messenger's high, she knew, and though it felt like freedom, it was really the melding with, the clicking in, that did it. The bike between her legs was like some hyper-evolved alien tail she'd somehow extruded, as though over patient centuries; a sweet and intricate bone-machine, grown Lexan-armored tires, near-frictionless bearings, and gas-filled shocks. She was entirely part of the city, then, one wild-ass little dot of energy and matter, and she made her thousand choices, instant to instant, according to how the traffic flowed, how rain glistened on the streetcar tracks, how a secretary's mahogany hair fell like grace itself, exhausted, to the shoulders of her loden coat."

—**William Gibson,** *Virtual Light*

"My legs and a silly something in me cry out for knocking the milestones down one by one and stopping at nothing. For years I have been telling myself that it's not the miles in the life that count but the life in the miles, but still this silly restlessness hurries me on."

—**Harold Elvin,** *The Ride to Chandigarh*

"I like to go fast, and use my brakes as little as possible."
—**Frank McCormack**

"The speeds that the end of June and the beginning of July brought, Jesse had never felt before, and he didn't trust them to last, didn't know if they could: and he tried to stay with the other riders, but didn't know if there was anything he could do to make the little speed he had last, in the curves, and that feeling, pounding up the hills, his heart working strong and smooth, like the wildest, easiest, most volatile thing ever invented."
—**Rick Bass,** *The Watch*

"I want to break the world record for slowness, to be by a long shot the last one there, to wish this bicycle a quarter inch off the ground so that together we become a single stationary beast under which the earth turns leisurely, bringing the finish line beneath me as I hang motionless, suspended through nebulae of gnats and subtle barometric changes, as close as I can come to that passion where there is no difference between the willed absence of motion and the still absolute of speed."
—**Claire Bateman,** "The Bicycle Slow Race"

"A stage racer practically lives on the bike. The sprinter truly lives for only a few minutes."
   —Davis Phinney

"I'm fascinated by the sprinters. They suffer so much during the race just to get to the finish, they hang on for dear life in the climbs, but then in the final kilometers they are transformed and do amazing things. It's not their force per se that impresses me, but rather the renaissance they experience. Seeing them suffer throughout the race only to be reborn in the final is something for fascination."
   —Miguel Indurain

"If you brake, you don't win."
   —Mario Cipollini

"Anybody can push down. That's natural. You walk up hills, you walk up steps. But cycling is unlike any sport I can think of. There is no other sport that requires picking up the leg up so fast. That's where the real art of sprinting is."
   —Mike Kolin

"For all their fearlessness, sprinters are a delicate breed. At the peak of form they effuse an aura of invincibility, suggesting no bicycle rider ever pedaled as fast. To win, sprinters must have everything: physical condition, confidence, luck, aggression and committed team support. An elusive combination, attainable but not sustainable."

—**David Walsh,** *Inside the Tour de France*

"You have to maintain a certain posture as a sprinter. To have a place at the head of affairs, where it is really dicey, I have to exude a confidence and strength so people won't mess with me."

—**Davis Phinney**

"I don't like rubbing shoulders with the other sprinters. I make my team ride at the front so that I can avoid physical contact with the others. I don't like taking risks."

—**Mario Cipollini**

"I like a power sprint much more than anything. I get freaked out in the big field sprints. I don't like bumping elbows with people."

—**Alison Dunlap**

"You have to sprint on feeling, not thinking. You must have faith in yourself but you cannot think about it too much."

—**Jean Paul Van Poppel**

"Since sprinting is the most explosive and volatile, the personalities reflect this. I like the danger and the speed. It brings out this primal feeling. It's like pushing the adrenal button."

—**Davis Phinney**

TRAINING

"Often I was in the saddle, so to speak, from morning till evening. I rode everywhere and usually at a good clip. Some days, I encountered some of the six-day riders at the fountain in Prospect Park. They would permit me to set the pace for them along the smooth path that led from the Park to Coney Island."

—**Henry Miller,** *My Bike and Other Friends*

TRAINING

One spring I got tired of being the world's worst sprinter, so I decided to start training for a big race at the end of the summer at the Lehigh Valley Velodrome. A velodrome is a huge oval (333 meters around at Lehigh) with banked walls that you ride on a bike with no brakes, no shifting and no way to coast. You can get either really fast or really hurt.

My coach was Alaric Gayfer, a cyclist who'd raced on the track, then retired to coach and work in the bike industry. He was funny, crude, loud, canny, still pretty fast and English, which is a great combination for a track coach. He'd stand by the start line in the infield and slowly spin to watch us as we pedaled around the track. High up on the wall in turn two, my front wheel drafting an inch behind two faster riders who were dicing around to keep me from diving under them—and watching over my shoulder for someone behind to start a dive under me— I'd hear Alaric's voice booming across the track to me: "Biiilllll. . . ." and then he'd shout something else.

But I could never tell if his instruction was, "Go noooowwww," or "Not nooooowwwwww," or "Go doowwwnnnnn." So, with my eyeballs bleeding because my heart was pumping so much blood through my body, and with my lungs threatening to open up my chest, I'd pick a strategy and do something. Anything.

When I'd get nipped at the line by faster guys who Alaric thought I could beat, he'd usually just shake his head, turn away and walk over to give wise, quiet advice to someone else. But sometimes we'd have a more detailed discussion. He'd stand right where he was, and as I soft-pedaled around the infield trying to remember my name and why I was on this planet, he'd boom: "Wot 'appened, Biillll?"

I'd fight my way out of oxygen debt and replay the disaster until I could say something like, "He came over me on the last turn and led everyone past."

And Alaric would shout, "Why?"

Everyone could hear all of this. I'd say, "Um, because I jumped too soon and gave him my draft halfway around the track?"

"Why?"

"I guess I thought I could outride him and he couldn't catch my draft."

"Why?"

"I just—I just thought I was faster."

"Why?"

"I don't uh . . . I really . . . I don't know."

And then he'd shake his head and turn away and walk over to give wise, quiet advice to someone else.

I never became the world's best sprinter, but I stopped being the worst. I even won a bronze medal in the big race, under lights, with the bleachers full and a pack of friends cheering me from turn four. But when I think of that summer at the velodrome the thing I recall most vividly is Alaric screaming at me, and how I responded with more speed and cunning when I was sure I had none. And I remember the wonderful regimen and ritual of training, getting up to be at the track at seven in the morning, driving out there with a friend or two and getting on the bike when there was still a chill to the air, and how at the end of the summer I could somehow scorch the riders who'd burned me all spring, and I remember a brilliant miss-and-out race I rode in training once and how afterward Alaric came over and told me I'd ridden as well as I could.

"The method is the same for you as it is for the pros. What is different is the workload."

—Michele Ferrari

"You need to let your form come. Tease it. All of a sudden you'll be riding, doing the same thing you've done for days, and you think: 'I'm going to go hard today.' You put it in the big ring and go, and you sustain it. Then you say, 'My god, I guess I am getting fitter.' That's the way it should be."

—Mike Neel

"Cycling takes so many hours to train and so many years to be really strong. Being good at cycling doesn't happen because you train hard one year."

—Rune Hoydahl

"I've always thought that it starts with genetics. It doesn't matter how hard you train, or how tough you are. Those are important, but you've got to have it in you to be a world-class athlete."

—Juli Furtado

"Once I begin serious training, eighty percent of the time I'll ride alone. Because you just can't say, 'I'll see you in a couple of minutes, I have to go anaerobic now.' So it's a lonely type of training. But you know what you have to do."
  —Phil Anderson

"Training is like Sisyphus pushing the boulder up the mountain only to have it roll back to the bottom. But if you do everything right, you get to balance the rock at the top one day a year."
  —Dave Scott

"You can't train luck."
  —Eddie B

"When you train better, you become a better rider. You have to push yourself to the limit—that's what makes the top riders. Some people can't do it, but that's what makes the good ones and the great ones."
  —Sean Kelly

"At the age of seven, I spent every day training."
   —Bjarne Riis

"I don't train. I just get anaerobic on the weekends and recover during the week."
   —Shaun Palmer

"I don't like to train. I would rather race. That's how I get into shape."
   —Miguel Martinez

"Golf pros hit balls on the range, swimmers practice with wooden paddles on their hands, and athletes in other sports do other things that improve performance by enhancing muscle memory. Too many cyclists just ride their bikes."
   —Mike Kolin

"I'm not going to be doing any Tour de Frances or big mountain bike courses, but it's good to mix things up."
   —Shaquille O'Neal, after custom-ordering the first
      bicycle that ever fit him

"I am told that men who compete in certain kinds of athletics—such as bicycle racing—shave their legs to prevent wind drag, and also to avoid getting their hair caught in the chain."

 —Abigail van Buren, answering a question to "Dear
  Abby" about male leg-shaving

"The velodrome is a microscope where you can tune your body and perfect your form."

 —Craig Griffin

"Some of the best bike riders in the world are BMXers. No one else has technical skills like theirs—except trials riders, and they do it at 5 mph. BMXers do it at any speed."

 —John Tomac

"BMX is the breeding ground for the next superstars of mountain biking."

 —Craig Barrette

"Lon came home from his ride wearing a trash bag the other day. I get so mad when he does that. We've got all these trash bags lying around that we never use."
—Susan Notorangelo-Haldeman

"I tell racers they should not be dependent upon anything. Not on drugs, not on their coach. The biggest trouble in life comes if you lose confidence in your character and in your capacities. I encourage the riders to be themselves. I try to give them more knowledge. I tell them to develop stronger personalities, to accept their own limitations."
—Paul Koechli

"People write and call and ask me to describe a general training week. But they don't need my general training week, they need their general training week. They need to figure their ideal training situation."
—Ned Overend

"You have to be flexible relative to the environment. The training is sport-specific in that your sport, mountain biking, is never specific—there are so many variables."
—David Farmer

"Ride lots."
   —Eddy Merckx

"Compare yourself to yourself. That's the most satisfying way to achieve improvement."
   —Mary Jane Reoch

"It's hard to measure yourself if nobody is challenging you."
   —John Tomac

"The worst thing you can do is try to be like Davis Phinney or Greg LeMond or anyone else. Make up your own mind about how you need to train—don't do what others do. You're ultimately responsible for yourself."
   —Mike Engleman

"There's no reason you have to classify yourself as one kind of bike rider. If you're built like a rail and you climb, why not develop speed or other skills you aren't good at?

Never stop working on your weaknesses."
   —Mike McCarthy, who transformed himself from a
      road racer to a world champion pursuit rider

"I know that I'm built for hills. But you don't have to be equally light to do well in this sport. What is important is to find the particular part of cycling that you're good at— whether it's climbing or sprinting—and use that as the basis for your style. Then you can go ahead and work on your weaknesses."
   —Atle Kvalsvoll

"Good advice comes from people who know what they're doing. Don't listen to anyone who's doing it wrong."
   —Myles Rockwell

"Know your own condition; never overextend yourself; always get enough sleep; never overeat; be regular in everything; exercise; relax; think positive thoughts."
   —Frank Kramer

"At the beginning stages, it is definitely the total physical development that is important. Later on you develop more mental concentration, mental preparation to maintain the physical capacity. Next you develop the spiritual."
—**Eddy Merckx**

"Basic physical strength is necessary. The body, legs and muscles have to be there. But you stay on bikes for hours and hours, so you need to have a little imagination. You need to be intelligent and calm. You need mental control. It is self-control."
—**Felice Gimondi**

"Pedaling is the essence of our sport. Everyone thinks I'm small-gear crazy, but pedaling fast for long periods helps develop the proper neuromuscular pathways. You must learn how to pedal quickly, then you can slow it down and develop power. Don't start by teaching yourself to pedal slowly because it's a hard process to reverse."
—**Mike Walden**

"Spinning will help the muscles develop elasticity. This is the quality which permits you to change the rhythm of your legs

instantly, something that is essential for success in racing. Spinning is an individual thing. It should be at a rate you can comfortably maintain. But no matter how fast you spin it is incorrect if your foot loses the sensation of the pedal."
—**Francesco Moser**

"By mid-March you should be living in the big chainring."
—**John Cobb**

"Ride a bike, ride a bike, ride a bike."
—**Fausto Coppi**

"I have no idea how many miles, how many hours, days, how fast, how much climbing I do. I couldn't imagine the prison of being a pro."
—**Carol Waters**

"Having all the sports-science knowledge in the world, having all the best coaches, having all the best equipment, will that win a gold medal for you? No. But not having all that can lose it for you."
—**Chris Carmichael**

"To win a classic is like winning the national lottery. But with the training I prescribe, the rider has two tickets in his pocket instead of just one."
—Francesco Conconi

"It's not a science. It's a war."
—Mike Neel

"For me it's very important to listen to what my body is saying. Once the season is under way I decide how to train from week to week by listening to how my body is feeling."
—Rune Hoydahl

"Biomechanics and all that knee-over-the-pedal plum line stuff is fine and dandy, but when it comes to saddle position, how you feel on the bike is what counts."
—David R. Farmer

"Most athletes treat their bodies like dead matter, lugging themselves through training schedule after training schedule. Training is both perplexing and sublime. Your body moves too slow (aging, etc.) and too fast (hormone activity etc.) to comprehend at just the cerebral level. It's dynamically more flexible and open to suggestion than you can imagine. You have to breathe and feel it, ponder it and then create a marriage of senses. This is the harmony of the true athlete. No coach can teach you but a good one can help you on your way."

—John Brady

"Ninety-five percent of the mountain bikers now—if you're talking top level—are training on their road bikes. It's much easier to get fit on the road because mountain biking can be inconsistent and you get so beat up and your whole body will get sore and cut up. It's also much more easy to crash and get injured on a mountain bike. Once you have fitness it's easier to get technique, not the other way around."

—Henrik Djernis

"I'm not one of those guys who rides a road bike all week and then races a mountain bike on the weekend. I don't enjoy riding road bikes. I wish I could do nothing but epic mountain bike rides and race on the weekend, but I can't."

—Dave Wiens

"I'm not into theory. I didn't have what you'd call a sterling scholastic career. I didn't even finish high school. I got my coaching philosophy hanging around the stables. You cared for the horses, washed them, walked them, and gave them massages. Every morning you took them out for training. Then you brought them back, gave them a bath and new straw, or maybe hot oats for the sick ones. With riders, it's exactly the same."
   —Mike Neel

"I learned the old school of cycling, where the more it hurts the better."
   —Jorg Muller

"Most recreational riders tend to cycle the same all the time: too hard most days, and too easy on hard days."
   —Michele Ferrari

"The training I like to do is go hard when you can, and when you do go hard you go as hard as you can."
   —Alex Stieda

"So many people have been sucked into the idea of high-quality, high-intensity training. They end up in never-never land, always going hard but not hard enough to gain speed. I give people permission to go slow. The body needs lots of low-intensity training, with focused high-intensity work."
—**Tom Ehrhard**

"I used to train too much, too many hours. In my first year as a pro I trained thirty-five hours a week, which is too hard."
—**Tony Rominger**

"I have a theory that intelligence decreases with fatigue. Whenever I was really tired, I could not tell if I needed to train more or not. That is the explanation I offer to explain why some people overtrain."
—**Norm Alvis**

"The truth is, you have to overtrain. It's a fallacy that you can stay rested all the time."
—**Steve Johnson**

"Overtraining is the disease of excellence."
   —William P. Morgan

"A slump is like a freight train. You always know when one hits."
   —Leonard Harvey Nitz

"To be a cyclist is to be a student of pain. Sure the sport is fun with its seamless pacelines and secret singletrack, its post-ride pig-outs and soft muscles grown wonderfully hard. But at cycling's core lies pain, hard and bitter as the pit inside a juicy peach. It doesn't matter if you're sprinting for an Olympic gold medal, a town sign, a trailhead, or the rest stop with the homemade brownies. If you never confront pain, you're missing the essence of the sport."
   —Scott Martin

"When I work out I make sure that I hurt. If there's no discomfort in it I ask myself why the hell I'm doing it."
   —Carol Waters

"You can't get good by staying home. If you want to get fast you have to go where the fast guys are."
 —**Steve Larsen**

"Why is it that when cross-country racers go out and ride the course they're training, but when the downhillers do the same they're practicing?"
 —**Zapata Espinosa**

"You've got to rest as hard as you train."
 —**Roger Young**

"The Tour is won in bed."
 —**Anonymous** wisdom on rest and recuperation

"When I say rest, I don't mean lying on the beach drinking beer. Rest is rest from bike, not rest from training."
 —**Eddie B**

"I'm going to sleep when I need sleep and train when I feel up to it."

—Laurent Jalabert

"From the dawn of humankind's existence we've sought ways to make time stand still. In our quest for the fourth dimension we've dehydrated ourselves in sweat lodges, and ingested hallucinogenic plants. We've even fantasized about building machines that could take us backward through time. But nothing makes the clock tick more slowly than stationary cycling."

—Don Cuerdon

"I'll wait for global warming before I'll ride a windtrainer through an entire winter. It's like pedaling through a huge bowl of oatmeal while someone takes the Jaws of Life to your bicycle. Not to mention the added tortures of not going anywhere, not seeing anything, and annoying your family by simulating the real-life sounds of a tornado in your own home."

—Christopher Koch

"I try to take care of myself by eating really well, avoiding sugar and soda and junk. It gives me an edge. If I didn't have that goddamn latte I wanted for three months, then I deserve to win the goddamn race."

—Missy Giove

"To prepare for a race there is nothing better than a good pheasant, some champagne and a woman."

—Jacques Anquetil

"No rider I know gets by after a raging ride with a bagel and a banana. That we could is irrelevant. Food is life, and if we are what we eat, I don't want to be a squishy, yellow fruit."

—Allison Glock

"It's okay to eat almost anything you want as long as you do not eat too much of it. Remember that you will pay for everything. If you eat too many grams of fat you must train that much more to get rid of them."

—Tony Rominger

"There are two things I eat that I know I shouldn't: chocolate and ice cream. You only live once, so I am going to eat chocolate."
—**John Tomac**

"When you're a pro bike racer so much of your life is machine-like. You cannot eat that way, too, because it weakens your motivation."
—**Jorg Muller**

"I have told Major Taylor that if he refrains from using liquor and cigarettes, and continues to live a clean life, it will make him the fastest bicycle rider in the world."
—**Louis Munger**

"Riders are not ducks, so they shouldn't drink plain water."
—**Eddie B**

"It's pretty standard to drink a Coke or coffee before an event. Racing in Europe, you really get caught up in it, especially cappuccino and espresso. It's an ambiance thing

as much as it is a performance enhancer."
   —Len Pettyjohn

"You begin by taking a sugar cube, then coffee, then some chocolate and from then on it's like a frenzy. You are drugged!"
   —Jacques Anquetil

"When you're turning the crankset, you're riding the bike. When you're coasting, you're just along for the ride."
   —Ned Overend, *Mountain Bike Like a Champion*

"You don't train today, you dream about being good."
   —Yuri Kasirin

"At the highest level of cycling there is no universal method of training. The approach to top form is one of the most complicated and mysterious—and yet simple—feats of sport. You ride your bike is all. But somewhere inside that is so much more."
   —Jan Kirstu

"The top riders are obliged to be fresh each time and they can't do that without stimulants. Nobody could or ever will be able to do that because there are no such things as supermen. Doping is necessary in cycling."

—**Rik van Steenbergen**

"My closets now will be empty of syringes and prohibited substances. The majority of racers have resorted to drug products, and those who refuse to admit it are liars."

—**Dietrich Thurau,** on his retirement

"Imagine someone telling you that by taking a certain drug you could win a single event and be three times richer, famous for life in your country—and it won't hurt anyone. What would you say? There's a wide range of ethics among the riders."

—**Ned Overend**

"I do not wish to hear spoken the word doping. Rather, one must say 'treating yourself,' and speak of treatments that are not appropriate for ordinary mortals. You cannot compete in the Tour de France on mineral water alone."

—**Jacques Anquetil**

"We prefer to dream about angels on wheels . . . somehow immune to the uppers and downers of our own pill-popping society. There is, all the same, a certain nobility in those who have gone down into God-knows-what hell in search of the best of themselves. We might feel tempted to tell them they should not have done it, but we can remain secretly proud of what they have done. Their wan, haggard looks are, for us, an offering."

—Antoine Blondin

FITNESS

"He was thinking about how it had been, when he had been in shape, and riding with the others, the pack: How his old iron bike had been a traitor some days, and his legs had laid down and died, and he had run out of wind—but how he had kept going, anyway, and how eventually— though only for a little while—it had gotten better."

—**Rick Bass,** *The Watch*

One day in 1994 I strapped on a full-face motorcycle helmet, then tapped the shoulder of a guy dressed in full leathers and gave him the thumbs up. He popped the clutch of the Beemer and we eased forward until we were even with the front of a blue start ramp that sat in the middle of the yellow stripes dividing a downtown street in Wilmington, Delaware.

I couldn't hear it over the roar of the moto, but I knew that an electronic speaker on the ramp was pulsing out low-toned beeps, one per second, and that when it gave a final, high-pitched beep we would shoot down the declining road at 35 or 40 miles per hour. Then the noise of the four-deep crowd surged over the Beemer's growl and Lance Armstrong exploded down the start ramp and we were off. I'd lucked into this spot on one of the Tour DuPont's follow vehicles and I wanted to make the most of it. I kept urging the driver forward until we were right behind Lance, even in front of the team car. I could see it all.

The speed was phenomenal, of course. You don't think anyone can really go that fast. It's almost not like cycling, it's so different from what most of us do on a bike. And then there was Lance himself. I'd been around a lot of pros—a few world champions, Tour de France and Paris-Roubaix winners, the best mountain bikers in the world—and watched a lot of races from behind barriers or in front of a television screen. I knew they were lean, with combustible muscles. I knew their skin lay tight over their bodies like shrink-wrap, making their quads and calves look even more swollen. But I'd never seen the leanness at work, not live, not just a few feet away. We pulled ahead of Lance and off to the side, and I could see his face. He was in terrible pain, but for him it was routine excruciating pain. Even though it tore at his body, he was smoother than I can ever hope to be.

Cycling allows no excess—no extra movement, wasted energy, unneeded weight. It punishes you for excess. Yet it is also one of the most forgiving sports, and this is how there can be a connection between the thoroughbred fitness of pro riders and the mongrel bodies of us recreational riders. Cycling does not batter your body like running or other high-impact sports. There are no spine-damaging torsions like there are in baseball or even golf. No sudden movements to rip cold muscles or tendons. People who are too heavy to participate in any other sport can ride because their weight is supported by the bike frame instead of their bodies.

At its upper level cycling rewards the hard, but at its lowest it welcomes the soft.

"Motivation can't take you very far if you don't have the legs."
   —Lance Armstrong

"Good morale in cycling comes from good legs."
   —Sean Yates

"Machines don't break records. Muscles do."
   —Lon Haldeman

"At times you ride on top of the world. Other times you feel you can't turn the pedals even once more. You've lost energy and you're not going to get it back. Then comes perseverance and going beyond what the physical body can do."
   —Ed Pavelka

"One of the reasons I ride is because it hurts at times. There's a certain discipline and freedom that comes when you push yourself to the limit. There have been times when my heart is about to jump out of my chest, my tongue is dragging in my spokes, and I'm sucking wind like a vacuum cleaner. And just when every nerve and fiber screams you can't do any more, somebody jumps and you take off after him, forgetting the pain. Later when you look inside yourself, you see things a little deeper, a little wider, and a little clearer. You realize that you can do things you never thought you could. Your dreams get a little bigger, your hopes a little stronger."
    —Rich Griffith

"It doesn't get any easier, you just get faster."
    —Greg LeMond

"I pedal my bike for only ten minutes and I'm exhausted. I don't know how those guys can ride for up to three hours."
    —Nicolas Vouilloz, comparing the all-out effort of
        downhill racing to cross-country's steady burn

"Cycling is unique. No other sport lets you go like that—where there's only the bike left to hold you up. If you ran as hard, you'd fall over. Your legs wouldn't support you."
   —Steve Johnson

"No doubt about it. Because of the power workouts and short, intense efforts, trackies have the biggest butts in the business."
   —Nancy Neely

"If you consider all-around fitness, mountain bikers have an edge. Road cyclists are so refined, like thoroughbred horses. They're unbelievably good at what they do—racing—but don't ask them to pull a plow."
   —Steve Tilford

"Many people think an athlete must look like a Greek god, but this isn't true as far as cycling goes. It's what's inside that counts. Nobody will ever know how little Gaul could pedal as fast as he could without blowing up, or what gave the tiny Ockers his tenacity. The things that go

toward making a great cyclist are big lungs and a slow-beating heart. . . . Size doesn't matter either. What does count is strength in relation to weight. You get all sorts, such as the late Gerard Saint, who was like a streak of nothing, or Robic, who was so short you couldn't see him in a bunch."
   —Ralph Hurne, *The Yellow Jersey*

"When I'm on my bike I forget about things like age. I just have fun."
   —Kathy Sessler

"Death may have no master, but the bicycle is, most emphatically, not its slave."
   —James E. Starrs, *The Noiseless Tenor*

"I'm a forty-two-year-old in a twenty-year-old's body."
   —Kent Bostick, after qualifying for the 1996 U.S.
      Olympic team against competition half his age

"Bike riding as little as three miles a day will improve your sex life."
   —Dr. Franco Antonini

"The truly extraordinary feature of the bike is that, like the very greatest teacher, it encourages you to find the answers from somewhere deep down inside yourself and not merely take them from someone else. When I began my adventure into myself on my bike I did not need to be told that I had to eat more of the right kind of food. I just knew I had to do it or else my legs would not work. I had never listened to or cared abut those long terrifying lectures about the evils of smoking—complete with colored slides of blackened lungs—but I did know, after some time in the saddle, that I just had to give up cigarettes. I did not need an expensive psychiatrist to tell me why I was depressed since, after a brisk ride, I was depressed no more."

—**Tom Davies**, *Merlyn the Magician and the Pacific Coast Highway*

"Fatigue is a disease and I don't want it."
—**John Marino**

"Most people tend to gauge their cycling progress in terms of 'how far?' or 'how fast?' But probably the most important question a rider can ask is 'How soon?' Recovery, your ability to recuperate from a cycling effort, is the most important indicator of overall fitness, but it's something people tend to ignore."

—Thurlow Rogers

"Cyclists worship legs. Your legs carry you over mountains, even when your mind and heart have long since abandoned the cause. Your legs—made solid by the miles—supply tangible evidence of your cycling progress. And your legs are what people notice at the beach."

—Nelson Pena

"Doctors can tell if they're operating on a cyclist just by looking at the internal tissues—they're strong and flexible, there's more muscle and less fat."

—Thomas Dickson

"For racers, it's common knowledge that the more fit you are, the less healthy you are. We always have to put on a jacket after a competition, even when it isn't cold, because if you catch just a little chill, you're gone."

—Connie Young

"What athletes do may not be that healthy, the way we push our bodies completely over the edge to degrees that are not human. I've said all along that I will not live as long as the average person."

—Lance Armstrong

"Knees have always been a cyclist's nemesis—the weakest link in the power train. Like a pitcher's elbow or a runner's hamstrings, when knees fail the activity can't continue."

—Andrew E. Slough

"Power. Think about the word. It is what separates casual riders from the elite. You can be a precision bike handler, a wheelsucker extraordinaire, an elegant pedaler—but if you can't crank when the crunch comes, you'll be left behind."

—Fred Matheny

"Power acts on cyclists the same way it does despots and dictators: It is intoxicating, addictive and, when carried to extremes, it can be destructive. With power, riding becomes fuller, more varied. It offers some of cycling's most wonderful sensations; the ability to ride up a hill faster than ever before, to take a turn at the head of a fast paceline, to feel the heightened awareness of blood pumping double time through every cell and the rhythm of breathing in sync with strong, steady pedal strokes. But with power, cycling also becomes more risky. It introduces a rider to overtraining and overuse."

—Christopher Koch

"Our bodies are like a car. When you drive a lot and drive very fast, you need more oil than a normal car."

—Jean-Paul van Poppel

"Some have heart like diesel, some have heart like Ferrari"

—Francesco Conconi

"So ardent a cyclist must be full of good health."

—Arthur Conan Doyle, "The Adventure of the Solitary Cyclist"

"I eat to ride, I ride to eat. At the best of moments, I can achieve a perfect balance, consuming just the right amount of calories as I fill up at bakeries, restaurants or ice cream parlors. On the road, I can get about twelve miles to the quart of milk and a piece of baker's apple tart."

—**Daniel Behrman,** *The Man Who Loved Bicycles*

"I get embarrassed when I see how slim I was."

—**Eddy Merckx**

RACING

"By George, here they came, atilting! Five hundred mailed and belted knights on bicycles!"
   —**Mark Twain**, *A Connecticut Yankee in King Arthur's Court*

Racing is such a tiny part of cycling. Somewhere around 50 million people ride bikes in America. About 34,000 have mountain bike racing licenses, and about 35,000 have road racing licenses. About 12,000 genetic freaks have both licenses, so that means out of 50 million bike riders only about 57,000 race—something around 0.114 percent, an amount comparable to a speck of grease on a bicycle. Even in Europe the racers are outnumbered by the commuters, the workers and the recreational riders.

Yet racing is cycling. Get on your bike and it begs you to race something—a friend, a dog, a leaf blown by the wind, your own best time, dusk, the approaching storm, the rider in the distance, your own mortality. Cycling is racing, and racing is brutal, beautiful, destructive, redemptive, awful and awe-full. You can find these qualities even when you're racing your shadow, but the pressure of organized races concentrates the feeling.

Any rider who's ever lined up beneath a start banner knows the delicious razored pain—some of us even like it—that afterward just leaves you feeling razored, as if the protective coating that shields us from life has been cut away, leaving us open to thoughts, perceptions, feelings and sensations we'd filter out on an ordinary day. Then there is the grace and ugliness found in every race (sometimes within pedal strokes of each other), what one of my friends calls the mosh ballet.

Soulful reasons aside, I suppose some of us pay entry fees to race because we like being recognized as winners, or to test ourselves or see where we stand among our friends and enemies. And I know some pros who do it simply because they are better at it than anything else, who do it for fame, or money, or both or all three.

But then there are so many more of us who for those same reasons choose not to dance on the razor in the mosh ballet. Their races aren't less important. Just more private. When you really think about it, that might be an even tougher place to find a victory.

"I remember seeing my first pro race. I was awed. I was awed by how many people were watching the race, a couple of hundred thousand spread along the course, and by how fit the riders were. They were like gods, so thin and fit. I couldn't believe how hard it looked."

—Greg LeMond

"There's a lot of feelings about racing you can never communicate. They're your own, and only you can identify with them."

—Alexi Grewal

"Cycling in general, and racing in particular, has a way of ordering and fulfilling our lives. When we get into cycling, we inherit a point of view, a perception, an attitude toward life."

—Owen Mulholland

"There's a feeling that you can only get from racing and finishing—the feeling of pushing yourself beyond what you're capable of doing in training. It's about achieving the ultimate physical accomplishment—and you can't feel that on the sidelines."

—Ned Overend

"While I am convinced the real draw of cycling is in its utility—the ability of the bike to move me from point A to B, I am equally convinced that competitive cycling is perhaps the penultimate use of the bike. The racer raises cycling to an aesthetic. He or she gives our sport its heroes and mythology."
—**James McCullagh**

"Bicycle road racing was the only sport in the world."
—**Ernest Hemingway,** *The Sun Also Rises*

"The great riders cannot exist without the lesser ones. I don't think the public realizes the protection given to the top riders. Everything is done for them. I don't think the public's imagination can grasp this. When you wait up a mountain for two or three hours it is marvelous to see what's happening at the front, but when you see the poor buggers struggling. . . . I feel more for them because they are putting more into it, because they have done all the donkey work as well. It's fantastic, really. That gives me the greatest thrill, seeing them and hoping they will make it inside the time limit."
—**Roger Yates**

"You have to taste the race. Unless you see it, experience the atmosphere, witness the riders' difficulties, then there will be no taste in the report. When you stay in the press room, you can't have this."

—Jarry Van den Bremt

"Scenery is something you can't take in. It's always there but you never see it, and neither do you notice the countless thousands of spectators whom you must pass in the course of the race. You can never be at ease and never let your mind wander for long from the race. Always you're too tired, too hot, too demoralized, too thirsty. The limit of your world is between the leading and tailing riders, and always there's the road in front, winding, ascending, dropping away."

—Ralph Hurne, *The Yellow Jersey*

"There's a sound of being in the middle of the pack. There's a big sort of rush."

—Alison Sydor

"People coming from a road background find the beginning of mountain bike races to be ballistic. You sit at the start for fifteen minutes, then your heart rate goes from eighty to a hundred and eighty instantly. Everyone's legs feel like cement, and you just go until you fade."
—Daryl Price

"Men invented war so they could be among themselves. In peacetime, they have bike racing."
—Gabriele Rolin

"To understand how satisfying it is to do well in racing, people need to understand how hard it is to push yourself in a race."
—Ned Overend

"I was so worked with one to go that I had to stop and ask this first-aid guy for something to eat. He gave me this crusty old peanut-butter sandwich, which was the only thing that saved me from death."
—Gene Oberpriller

"For me, it's like getting four root canals all at once: long, drawn-out agony."
   —**Sue Fish,** downhill racer, on cross-country mountain bike races

"I know how the pain of cycling can be terrible: in your legs, your chest, everywhere. You go into oxygen debt and fall apart. Not many people outside cycling understand that."
   —**Greg LeMond**

"The race was so painful. The riding wasn't hard but I crashed at least once a lap. I think I went down eight times."
   —**Norm Alvis,** making the change from pro roadie to pro mountain bike racer

"A mountain bike race is a constant hard effort for two to three hours. In road racing the efforts often come in surges. You ride easy for awhile then you have to make an extreme, hard effort. They are two different efforts, two different forms of suffering."
   —**John Tomac**

"When you're alone and you get to that weak point—when you get really tired and it's easy to quit—everything becomes clear. You get really honest with yourself. Whenever you break yourself down that far, you break your inhibitions down also. A lot of time you can fake it and cover it up. But at three in the morning of a 24-hour race, nothing is hidden."

—John Stamstad

"You really don't know why you feel so bad. That's what's so hard about mountain bike racing. You really can't tell. Are you being lazy? Undertrained? Overtrained? When you're in the middle of it you can't view yourself objectively, so you don't know what to do."

—Juli Furtado

"In the last seven years, I've had four months that I felt good. And in those four months I won two Tours de France and the world championships. But in the rest of those years I've just been struggling."

—Greg LeMond

"To me, cross-country racing is the mask of pain. You go out and suffer and see who's at the front. That's what I think of as a classic cross-country race—just the looks on the riders' faces. How hard it is to do is what makes it so satisfying a sport to be involved in."

—Ned Overend

"Racing isn't 'Boy, I feel great, everyone's falling over, I think I'll just ride away.' That's not it at all. If you're just not sick and your tires are full, you can't ask for anything more."

—Andy Hampsten

"As I see one ancient charm after another fall victim to that mindless beast known as commercial progress, it's heartening to know that the cyclocross cultists are out there holding on to the history that's important to them. It's a relic worth preserving."

—Zapata Espinoza

"I watch videos of cyclocross races, and over and over I review the parts where people hop off and on their bikes, run with their bikes. It's so graceful, almost like gymnastics."

—Shari Kain

"I like cyclocross because it's a spastic scurry just like my life."

—Lisa Muhich

"When I think about a cyclocross race the main thing that comes to mind is the beauty of it all (once you get past the pain). The physical grace of the riders as they get off their bikes; just as you think they're going to become another barrier casualty, they just seem to float over the obstacles and then are back on their bikes before you can even blink. Beautiful."

—Pineapple Bob

"The bicycle riders drank much wine, and were burned and browned by the sun. They did not take the race seriously except among themselves."

—Ernest Hemingway, *The Sun Also Rises*

"Today, Fabio will be on his bike beside and within me, and like that all the way to Paris. He'll be with me in the month ahead. All my life, he'll be with me."

—Andrea Peron, after teammate and roommate Fabio Casartelli died in the 1995 Tour de France

"I loved the course today, but I felt so cramped in my style. That's what I don't like about racing—you have to conform your style and be conservative so you don't crash."

—**Myles Rockwell**

"There are very few real leaders. They may think of themselves as leaders but through the eyes of their equipiers they are not."

—**Eddy Schepers**

"I threw up on the first climb. Racing is always hard when your breakfast is in your throat."

—**Thomas Frischnecht** at the '99 World Cup
Cross-Country Race, in Napa, California

"If you've never watched a race, don't. Just enter."

—**Jacquie Phelan**

"I don't race because I get a euphoria out of cycling a lot of people probably don't. Besides, I can't sprint."

—**Jobst Brandt**

"In the beginning, one man raced alone against history. The world figured he was an oddball, if it could figure him at all."
—**Robert P. Laurence**

"Small races are the time to experiment with pace, equipment and nutritional supplements. Too many people are so serious about races that they won't experiment."
—**Ned Overend**

"I must write the strange world of the six-day races and the marvels of road racing in the mountains. French is the only language it has ever been written in properly and the terms are all French and that is what makes it hard to write."
—**Ernest Hemingway,** *A Moveable Feast*

"Competition is painful and wonderful and insane and ugly and beautiful, beautiful, beautiful. Forget magazines and how-to books. The fastest, best way to become a better mountain biker is to race. The fastest, best way to get in touch with the pure physical exhilaration and hardship of this sport is to race. The fastest way to go faster is to race."
—**Dan Koeppel**

"Racing for me acts as a form of meditating. It raises my self-esteem and gives me great satisfaction—just knowing that I'm overcoming big odds and doing something that most women wouldn't do. I'd rather be out riding my bike than shopping in a mall!"

—**Kathy Sessler**

"Some people are professional trainers and do little racing. But you can make the greatest gains through competition. I never would have realized my potential if it weren't for racing. There's nothing like it to push you. It improves fitness and bike handling. You find yourself at speeds you would never attain in training."

—**Ned Overend**

"Racing, on any level, seeks a balance within us. For every moment of hassle and pain, there is one of revelation and joy. For my money, I'll take the bad road food with the good sunsets, the injured weak days with the winning sprints, and the long hot drives with the two hours of playing in the dirt. Is it worth it? Always."

—**Mike Ferrentino**

WINNING AND LOSING

"You set out in company with your own ability and fate. There are the good bits and the bad, the easy and the hard. You climb, descend, slog, rest. Very occasionally you win. Other than the winner, you all go unnoticed and unappreciated and are soon forgotten. Winners are always remembered."

—**Ralph Hurne,** *The Yellow Jersey* '

Is a win always better than a loss?

Winning is rarer—because while anyone can lose, only a few people ever win something that really counts. And winning certainly feels better—and earns you more prize money if you're a pro. But even at the pro level, a loss full of honor and courage can reap more acclaim (and sponsorship exposure) than an ordinary victory.

My greatest loss means more to me than any win.

In 1994 my wife, Beth, three friends and I entered West Virginia's 24 Hours of Canaan mountain bike race. It's a team relay in which each rider does a lap then hands a baton off to the next rider, rotating continuously from noon Saturday to noon Sunday. There was 1,800 feet of vertical gain each lap, including a two-mile dirt-road climb to the high point, from which you dropped into a single-track plunge across jagged rock fields, slimy roots, mucked waterholes, and handlebar-width gaps between trees. Each rider does four to six laps of this (depending on how fast your team is), including a couple at night when your world shrinks to the dimensions of the tiny bubble of light your headlamp casts and you ride things you cannot see. All while you become progressively more fatigued, sleepy and malnourished.

My first lap had been our team's fastest, one hour and seventeen minutes. But as the race wore on my times slowed to 1:21 and then 1:32. On Sunday morning, one hour and twenty-one minutes before noon, my turn came up. Everyone—including me—agreed there was no way I could finish before noon, so my lap would be our last. They began showering and changing into nonriding clothes while I staggered into the first climb.

I had nothing. And maybe that was why I began riding like I never had before—or have since. Flying. Carving. Not caring. At the crest I saw Beth, who'd ridden the chairlift up to snap photos. "Fourteen minutes to the end!" she shouted as I whooshed by. A caution I heard as a cheer. As I approached the finish area our teammate Mike ran toward me screaming, "Don't cross the line!" But I heard, "You have a great line!"

I finished the best ride of my life at 11:58 a.m., disqualifying my team because technically we'd quit racing before noon. I was a loser, but for an hour and nineteen minutes I'd become the rider I dreamed of being when I was a kid. I'd lose for the rest of my life if I could ride like that again.

"The race is always won by a strongman. The truth comes through the pedals."
   —**Laurent Jalabert**

"It was eleven more than necessary."
   —**Jacques Anquetil,** after winning a race by
      twelve seconds

"I was very lucky, because the others were better than me."
   —**Francois Faber,** after winning the 1913 Bordeaux-
      Paris race by twenty-two minutes

"It was kind of a lonely ride with lots of time to think about winning. But I told myself to concentrate on the job—there would be time to celebrate later."
   —**Alison Sydor,** on her world championship in 1994

"The Europeans look down on raising your hands. They don't like the end-zone dance. I think that's unfortunate. That feeling—the finish line, the last couple of meters—is what motivates me."
   —**Lance Armstrong**

"I thought I was ahead the whole time. Then I saw my boyfriend going crazy in the infield, and I knew it must be close, so I sprinted."
—**Rebecca Twigg,** on her 1992 Olympic pursuit gold medal

"When you get second place, you say 'I could have won it here, I could have won it there.' When you win, you never say anything; it's finished."
—**Greg LeMond**

"To win races, you have to cultivate friendships."
—**Davide Boifave**

"I win less often than Fondriest, but when I win it's historic."
—**Claudio Chiappucci**

"Anyone interested in winning Olympic gold medals must select his or her parents very carefully."
—**Per-olof Astrand**

"Age and treachery will overcome youth and skill."
   —Fausto Coppi

"He's dancing on the pedals in an immodest way!"
   —Phil Liggett, on a victory by Dag-Otto Lauritzen

"I was a hero, and a second afterwards it was all over. Casartelli was dead so what I had achieved was worth nothing."
   —Richard Virenque, on winning the Tour de France
        stage in which Fabio Casartelli died in a crash

"Now the *maglia rosa* is mine. I believe I've earned it. I'm happy to have won it on the most difficult stage I've ever ridden in my life. Today, my life has changed."
   —Pavel Tonkov, after winning the Giro d'Italia by
        dropping race leader Abraham Olano on the
        final, 13-km, 18-percent climb

"It's a viciously cruel sport."
   —Phil Liggett

"Evidently one does not need an aptitude for this job."
—**Ottavio Bottecchia,** after winning his first race

"I guess I just have bigger ovaries."
—**Missy Giove**

"I love winning, but I also love being consistent."
—**Tinker Juarez**

"My wife has reproached me for dedicating my victories to everyone in the world except her. So I owe her this one. Especially because living with someone like Mario Cipollini is very tough."
—**Mario Cipollini**

"I'm the reference point. If they beat me, they win."
—**Miguel Indurain**

"A win is a win. Only you can win normally or you can win with panache."
—**Eddy Merckx**

"I don't need to win by three or four minutes. I just want to make it across that finish line first—three minutes, three seconds, three one-hundredths-of-a-second, it's all the same, really."
—Tinker Juarez

"Winning is a matter of training and tranquillity."
—Alex Zulle

"It is important to win, but more than anything it is important to always be at the front, to be a factor in every race, to be somebody that everybody respects and looks for."
—Francesco Moser

"I like to win but I'm not motivated to win. I never go into a race saying, 'I want to win this.' The thing that motivates me is riding for someone, either leading out a sprinter or helping a climber or defending a jersey. And when I'm in that situation, in any of those situations, then I perform much better because I'm motivated."
—Sean Yates

"Mental preparation makes all the difference in the world between being a good rider and a rider who wins."
   —Leonard Harvey Nitz

"I won because I was smarter. [Mauro] Gianetti was stronger, but I was smarter. It's important to race with your head."
   —Johan Museeuw, after sitting in behind Gianetti
      on the last lap of the world championship, then
      outsprinting him at the line

"I would trade any result this year for a gold medal. But they don't accept trades in Atlanta."
   —Lance Armstrong

"A win will make a big head even bigger."
   —Gert Jakobs

"I race to win, not to please people."
   —Laurent Fignon

"In bicycle racing the finish line is sometimes merely the symbol of victory. All sorts of personal triumphs take place before that point, and the outcome of the race may actually be decided long before the end."

—Laurence Malone

"I love mountain biking. There's no hiding, like there can be with road racing. We're all out on our own. The strongest rider almost always wins the race."

—Alison Dunlap

"One thing cycling taught me was that if you can achieve something without a struggle it's not going to be satisfying."

—Greg Lemond

"I was the first Olympic medalist I ever knew."

—Curt Harnett

"After Francesco Moser set the hour record, someone asked him if he spun a small gear or pushed a big gear. He said, 'I spin a big gear.' I figured, so that's how you win on the track."

—Jane Quigley

"Do not give up when you find that you have to suffer greatly in order to get results. Never forget that the winners are the ones who can suffer best. It's the no-hopers who cannot suffer. The inability to suffer is almost always the real reason riders do not succeed in our sport. He who can suffer best has the best chance to get to the top."

—**Charles Ruys**

"I think that was the most significant event in my life, standing up there and getting that medal that I had worked so hard for. Everyone, at least once in their life, should have an opportunity to feel like that. I felt like Miss America."

—**Greg Herbold** on winning 1990 world downhill championship

"There's a terrible delight in watching a rival sink without a trace."

—**Bernard Hinault**

"Once you flat, the pressure's off. At the start of a race, there's a lot of pressure to win. But once you flat, you figure, hey, you got your excuse for not winning, you might as well just go for it. It's a nice way to ride."

—Ned Overend

"There are no races. Only lotteries."

—Jacques Anquetil

"There are some riders who will win, and there are others who will not win. It is not difficult to see which is which."

—Eddy Schepers

"I am not a bad loser. It is probably a fault. Rarely do I feel down after losing. But I take the victories very much in my stride as well, not being able to enjoy the moment of success as much as others. My aim has always been to be a good professional. When I sit down and try to work out my attitude to winning and losing it comes out thus: I am not a bad loser, it is just that I prefer to win."

—Stephen Roche

"The whole thing reminded me of a bad New Year's Eve party. You have all these great expectations built up, then you go home feeling let down."

—**Charlie Livermore,** on the American performance at the first mountain bike Olympic race

"I was more relieved than anything. People were sick of me winning—I don't blame them. It's hard when you win all the time, because then winning isn't special anymore."

—**Juli Furtado,** after finishing second to end a winning streak of seventeen of eighteen races in 1993, including all six national championship series races and nine World Cup races

"When you abandon, the festival continues without you. You are physically weak and you feel rejected. This feeling of exclusion hurts far more than the physical pain."

—**Bernard Hinault**

"My big luck was to have lots of bad luck."

—**Raymond Poulidor**

"I felt really good that day. I was sure I would have won if my seat had not fallen off."
—**Francois Gachet,** after placing ninth in the 1993
world championships

"I really did believe I could win. Look at my head. I visited the barber's shop this morning for a haircut to get ready for the winner's photo."
—**Erik Breukink,** after finishing 33rd at Fleche
Wallone in 1994

"I tried to follow Riis three times and the fourth time I gave up. Riis was very strong, so strong that he was climbing on the big ring when I was climbing on the thirty-nine ring. It's on the day when you lose the favorite that you lose the Tour. The gap with Riis is unbridgeable unless he blows. After twelve years my body just can't do any more. It was a day which had to come."
—**Miguel Indurain,** on getting cracked in stage 16 of
the 1996 Tour de France, interrupting his
string of five consecutive victories

"Indurain knows how to lose like a champion."
—**Spanish newspaper headline**

"Refrain from throwing your bicycle in public. It shows poor upbringing."
—Jacquie Phelan

"I think that for any professional racer, the jersey of a national champion is most important. The French jersey is a beautiful one to wear."
—**Gerard Rue,** after a teammate led a chase that caught his solo breakaway with half a lap remaining and cost him the 1992 French championship

"I gave it all I had, got dropped, and rode in to give another day. But it's hard. It's hard to have everybody see you back there. It's more than a little embarrassing, but that's what being a professional is all about."
—**David Farmer,** on being dropped in the Tour DuPont

"It was the first time in my career that I've finished in the laughing group. I saw the ass of guys whom I have never seen the face of."
—**Alex Zulle,** after a bad stage in the 1995 Tour of Spain

"The broom wagon never moves up the long parade to seek a lagging rider. But if the last rider drops to the very rear, the van will remain a few feet behind him. To some, that might suggest a shark trailing a shipwreck survivor on a raft."

—Sam Abt

"There is nothing in my legs. I look for a place to end it. A place void of people so that I can retire with dignity. I stop on the right hand side of the road after a kilometer of climbing. I have cracked. It is over. The broom wagon and ambulance stop behind me. I stand, head bent down over my bike, as a nurse descends from the ambulance and offers her sympathies. A commissaire gets out of the broom wagon and unpins the two race numbers from my back. 'C'est dure,' (it's hard), he sighs, as he completes this unpleasant duty. People further up the mountain come running down to witness the excitement. There are ohs and ahs as I climb into the bus, and then cheers as I am driven away. I feel numb and dazed and cold."

—Paul Kimmage, on abandoning the Tour de France

"No excuses."

—Ted Smith

CRASHES

"There is no reason why a man on a smooth road should lose his balance on a bicycle; but he could."
  —**C.S. Lewis,** *Perelandra*

There are two rules about bike crashes:

1. They happen.
2. They inspire stories.

Simple, huh? Everything else is negotiable. Crashes can be spectacular or boring. Funny or tragic. They are our fault, they are our fate. It was the bike, it was the earth, it was the idiot in front of you. You ride away unscraped, you twist and writhe in pain, or lie there silent and unmoving. It is bloody, it is muddy. You learn from it or you repeat it. You learn from it and you repeat it. Life becomes a slow-motion series of snapshots that flip past your eyes a million frames a second each one clear and distinct, or you are riding along and the next thing you see is the sky. You live or you die.

You can die on a bike. We cyclists rarely admit that; we say it aloud or write it even less. I don't think it's coincidence that most crash stories are funny. Even some of the true tragedies—a death wreck or a disability—over time come to include some light moment or aside that somehow adds rather than subtracts poignancy and reverence. I don't think this is callousness or disregard. I think it's a kind of protective reflex—like a blink after a long stare. I think it's hope. I think it's a kind of unspoken promise that we will keep riding, that we will remember why cycling is good.

One steamy summer at a race in West Virginia I tried to pass a rider by going off the singletrack, and T-boned some tombstone rocks sunk in a mudhole. After I flew over the handlebar I just laid there for a few seconds, letting the warm mud fold over me like a blanket. The sound of treads buzzing by my head was almost soothing. I could've taken a nap—and I think I started to until I felt something wet and warm spurting from the side of my neck. I am dying, I thought. So this is how it'll be. I slapped my hand against the pulsing gush and felt the plastic hose of my CamelBak— a backpack with a bladder you fill with water so you can sip from its hose instead of taking your hands off the handlebar to grab a bottle from its cage. When I wrecked, the nozzle had come off and released the flow of water.

I finished twenty-sixth out of fifty, just out of the top half, very thirsty, but happy to be alive.

"If you ride your bike, you might get hurt, you might become impotent, and, hell, you might even die. What to do? Ride your bike anyway."
—**Zapata Espinosa**

"Cat 5 racers crash by another's accident. Cat 1 racers crash by another's design."
—**Arnie Baker**

Falling is okay. What's not good is not knowing why you fell. Don't waste a perfectly good fall or you'll just have to do it again. Treat it as a physics lesson."
—**Tom Hillard**

"Falling comes easy to all of us, but falling properly is an art. If you train yourself to avoid the natural impulse to stick your hand out, you have a chance to tuck your shoulder in and roll. The force of landing is spread rather than concentrated on one small spot. This is a drill you can practice at home with couch cushions, mattresses, whatever. I'd recommend doing it about every six months, just to keep the feel."
—**Chris Carmichael**

"Falling down is the Esperanto of mountain biking. If you ride with any passion, you've wiped out. A good crash makes you blood brothers, members of a scarred and happy clan."
  —Allison Glock

"Road rash definitely doesn't preclude racing. Neither is it a badge of courage. Mostly, it is a red flag to the other riders regarding bike-handling ability."
  —Norm Alvis

"You need to know why you fall. It's how you learn. If you crash and you don't know why, that's the time to slow and relax awhile."
  —Hans Rey

"The way you learn, is you go around a corner and crash. Then you know that's too fast so the next time you go a little slower."
  —Ron Kiefel

"Suddenly the nickel-clad horse takes the bit in its mouth and goes slanting for the curbstone defying all prayers and all your powers to change its mind—your heart stands still, your breath hangs fire, your legs forget to work."

—**Mark Twain,** "Taming the Bicycle"

"If I have one of those days when I keep falling, I just say, 'Okay, slow down and enjoy the ride.' "

—**Ruthie Matthes**

"You don't really ever have to fall. But kissing ground is good because you learn you're not going to die if it happens."

—**Jacquie Phelan**

"We all know the old saying, 'Fire is a good servant but a bad master.' This is equally true of the bicycle: If you give it an inch—nay, a hair—it will take a yard—nay an evolution—and you a contusion, or, like enough, a perforated kneecap."

—**Frances Willard,** *How I Learned to Ride the Bicycle*

"The problem is that you can be wounded in your mind as well as your physique."
  —Marco Pantani

"If you want to be a pro, you should expect pain. Over and over. Be prepared for some serious soil sampling."
  —Myles Rockwell

"You don't feel pain after a crash, only mental anguish."
  —Marla Streb

"If I crash, I crash. If not, I should win."
  —Missy Giove

"If you're crashing a lot, you're just being stupid."
  —Greg Herbold

"Some people pay a thousand dollars for a tattoo. This scar cost me twenty grand."
  —Matt Hoffman

"Nobody ever died from not knowing how to play flag football. Yet we spend tax money teaching kids its nuances in gym classes, while bicycle safety is still foreign to most school curriculums. That ain't right."

—Don Cuerdon

"If we all, mountain bikers, cyclists, multinational companies, Jo Public, respected the land like old civilizations we wouldn't get so many punctures. Earth's revenge."

—Jo Burts

"Forget about your rights. Forget about what's fair. Forget all the rules of etiquette you ever learned. The average bicycle weighs twenty-five pounds. The average motorized vehicle weighs twenty-five hundred pounds. Your job is to avoid getting into an accident, not to prove you were within your rights after you're involved in one."

—Bob Katz

"The sound of a car door opening in front of you is similar to the sound of a gun being cocked."

—Amy Webster

"This bad luck is getting to me. I had two wheel changes, a big scare at the feed when I broke a wheel and nearly fell off, then I crashed coming down the last col. It's a bit much when you've been at the front all day."

—Tony Rominger

"My grandfather told me: Always wear underpants beneath your kanzu before you mount your bicycle. Foolishly I mocked him, and now my heart is a dry ear pod. I was cycling home from the market when a terrible whirlwind blew up my kanzu, ballooning it over my face and lifting me far above the ground. I kept control but when the bike landed I sat down hard upon my testicles, squashing them against the saddle to the flatness of patties. A sharp pain ran through my entire body. Then I felt an inner peace and went into a deep sleep."

—Mzee Opesen

"I came into the last gate at about thirty-five miles per hour and something hooked my pedal. The next thing I knew, the bike was turned 180 degrees around, and I was thrown backward sixty feet. I hit the timing pole with my hip and it popped out like a Ken doll's."

—Dave Cullinan, on his crash at the Hunter
    Mountain dual slalom

"I was feeling great and set to catch Greg LeMond when my brand-new freewheel skipped for the fourth time. The front wheel turned at a 90-degree angle and I flipped. My helmet flew off and they said you could hear my head hit the ground from a mile away. I decided I needed to make something, create something because life is short."

—**Gary Fisher,** on the 1979 Tour of Nevada City

"I hit a waterbar at 43 mph. I thought I could ride through it like I had in practice, but instead I kicked into a nose wheelie for 50 yards, then went over the bars. I punctured my lung and broke five ribs. There was a lot of loose skin."

—**Hans Rey,** on his crash at Hunter Mountain

"I leaned into the guy a little bit. I crowded him underneath. He was a small rider and he just clipped me under my elbow and upended me. When I crashed, I lost a lot of skin and was delirious from a concussion. I slid so hard on my head, the plastic on my helmet melted. Some people thought I'd broken my neck. Then, while I was lying on the track, another rider hit me at 45 mph, which caused the blood vessels in my lungs to burst."

—**Marty Nothstein,** on his crash at the Athens
velodrome in 1995

"I just launched over this waterbar, totally bad attitude, and I landed on my head. I had the splintered helmet, the backboard, I couldn't move. I was rushed to a hospital and taped down for two hours. My mind was racing. I was thinking, 'my life could change a lot.'"

—**Travis Brown**

"I lose the sense of balance, to the point Gaston Plaud and the mechanic had to support me for more than two hundred meters before I could start again. Finding my way, I had to climb the thread of my own existence to know who I was, and what I was doing on the bicycle. Then I saw the 'Peugeot' on my jersey and I remembered that I was a cyclist. But in what race were we? I didn't have any idea, until I noticed the Tour's yellow plate screwed on the bumper of the Peugeot's team car. Not being sure of anything, I am inquiring from Gaston Plaud who answered, 'Yes, we are in the Tour, don't worry, you fell on your head.'"

—**Bernard Thevenet,** Tour de France, 1972

"Not only did I break my seatpost, I also broke a nail."

—**Kathy Sessler**

"Someone in front of me misjudged a fairly straightforward bend. I was outside him and had to go a bit wider and just went straight into the ravine. At first I thought I was going to go all the way to the bottom of it, but fortunately the bushes were very thick and broke my fall. You have the impression that you are never going to stop, even if it lasts only a few seconds."

—**Johan Bruyneel,** on going over a cliff in the 1996
Tour de France

"Who am I? Where am I? Oh yes, I'm at the Tour so I should get on my bike and go. Where is my bike?"

—**Djamolidin Abdujaparov**'s first words after
regaining consciousness after a crash, 1996

"Put me back on my bike."

—**Tom Simpson**'s last words, in the 1967 Tour de
France after he fell from his bike

"Every rider crashes."

—**Eddie B.**

"You'll die at least five years sooner if you ride a single-speed mountain bike. You have to hurt a lot."
   —**Andrew Kempe**

"Momentum is the only thing you have to show for all your suffering. Don't waste it."
   —**Richard Cunningham**

"A crash is a hard as you make it."
   —**Greg Randolph**

"The secret is pretty simple. The slower you go the more likely it is that you'll crash."
   —**Juli Furtado**

"My head hit a tree, I did a whirly-bird into the crowd, and broke my full-face helmet. I knew I needed to quit. I think as you get older, a self-defense mechanism kicks in—like not wanting to die."
   —**Greg Herbold** on crashing in the 1995 world
      championships

THE FIRST RIDE

"After your first day of cycling, one dream is inevitable. A memory of motion lingers in the muscles of your legs, and round and round they seem to go. You ride through Dreamland on wonderful dream bicycles that change and grow."

—**H. G. Wells,** *The Wheels of Chance*

First we are floaters, swimmers in what William Kotz-winkle calls the "secret sea." Then we are bound to the ground, unable to even turn over. By degrees we gain mobility, strengthening our muscles and our coordination until we can sit up, then clamber to our hands and knees, then rock back and forth, then put those motions together into forward movement, and finally we grope our way to our feet and walk and it is wonderful but it is a battle against gravity the whole time.

We swim again, of course, but not the way we did before. The crawl and the dog-paddle so precisely describe our progress, the butterfly a laughable antonym of how we actually proceed through water.

It is not until we find the bicycle that we rediscover flight, the unstrained weightlessness we knew in the womb, the easy, lofting movements and sweeping curves possible with a subtle tilt of our bodies. The bicycle ride is something we remember from before we had memory, plus more. It is wind, it is a world of color to rush over and by and below, it is a world of friction yet freedom.

Humans were meant to ride bicycles, or else we could never accomplish the feat. Scientists cannot explain how a bicycle stays upright. There are too many forces and variables. We can shoot a metal can across our solar system but there are not enough mathematical formulas to explain how a six-year-old child rides a bike. The explanation is simple. The explanation is this: We already know how to ride bikes. We just need to remember it.

We never stop remembering how to ride a bike. There is always more to remember. There are finer and finer movements to make, the tiniest shifts of weight, imperceptible leans. There are tricks, ways to pedal or hold the handlebar, a stance for your knees as you ride over a log, an elbow movement that sucks up the impact of landing after a hop. When you become older and slower you can sometimes go faster than ever if you use everything you know about riding a bike.

It is always sweet for that reason, but never like the first time. Remember that first time. Remember how to ride. And remember, of course, how true it really is that we never forget how to ride a bicycle.

"If I am asked to explain why I learned the bicycle, I should say I did it as an act of grace, if not of actual religion."

—**Frances Willard,** *How I Learned to Ride the Bicycle*

"Get a bicycle. You will not regret it if you live."

—**Mark Twain,** "Taming the Bicycle"

"No matter how one may think himself accomplished, when he sets out to learn a new language, science, or the bicycle, he has entered a new realm as truly as if he were a child newly born into the world."

—**Frances Willard,** *How I Learned to Ride the Bicycle*

"To ride a bicycle properly is very like a love affair; chiefly it is a matter of faith. Believe you can do it and the thing is done; doubt, and for the life of you, you cannot."

—**H.G. Wells,** *The Wheels of Chance*

"I took a deep breath, looked for a final time at those comforting tires, pushed off and, to my amazement, actually went somewhere. I was awkward. I was ungainly. I hadn't gone more than three or four feet, but by God I felt the balance and that was enough. I did it!"

—**Ken Turan,** learning to ride at age forty-six

"A means of new life. Nothing else offered itself."

—**Henry Adams,** learning to ride at fifty, after the death of his wife

"Sighing for new worlds to conquer, I determined that I would learn the bicycle."

—**Frances Willard,** *How I Learned to Ride the Bicycle*

"I never had to use training wheels. When I was twelve, I got a Schwinn Collegiate and taped a six-volt battery to my top tube. I got Christmas tree lights on it and rode around my neighborhood singing Christmas carols."

—**Greg Bagni**

"The hardest part of raising a child is teaching them to ride bicycles. A shaky child on a bicycle for the first time needs both support and freedom. The realization that this is what the child will always need can hit hard."

—**Sloan Wilson**

"A childhood without a bicycle is a sailboat becalmed. A bicycle has the grace and style to give a billowing gaiety and a transcendent innocence to the fragile moments of childhood. In later years, those moments may be recalled for refuge, however evanescent, from the fits and frights of life."

—**James E. Starrs,** *The Noiseless Tenor*

"The bicycle is the steed that never tires, and is mettlesome in the fullest sense of the word. It is full of tricks and capers, and to hold his head steady and make him prance to suit you is no small accomplishment."

—**Frances Willard,** *How I Learned to Ride the Bicycle*

"Some things need to be drawn before they can be designed and understood. Others need to be made first, and the bicycle is the latter. It is inconceivable that the principles involved in riding a bicycle could ever be theorized first. It's far more likely that the principles of balance related to the bicycle were discovered by someone playing around with things that had wheels. Put simply, a cyclist proceeds in a series of falls that are compensated for by steering the bicycle back under the center of gravity. This complex principle cannot be analyzed by computers, but it's done automatically by us clever apes—and it is a skill once learned never forgotten."

—Mike Burrows

"The cyclist has acquired a new habit, an automatic unconscious habit, solely because he wanted to and kept trying until it was added into him."

—George Bernard Shaw, *Back to Methuselah*

"Most of us have tried to walk on the top rail of a fence and have a vivid recollection of the tossing of arms and legs to keep our balance and the assistance we got from a long stick or a stone held in our hands. But the cyclist gets no help. We must ask, then, how is it possible for one supported on so narrow a base to keep his seat so securely and, seemingly, so without effort? Gyration has nothing to do with it; centrifugal force has no application to it, except when turning corners, or otherwise changing abruptly the direction of the movement; balancing is a detriment rather than an assistance; and rapid motion alone accounts for nothing. Some other explanation is needed."

—*Popular Science,* 1891

"The moment a man bestrides a bicycle he becomes a horse with all the whims and mad prancings of that creature."
—**Octave Mirbeau,** *Sketches of a Journey*

"It is when you come back to bicycling, after long dispractice, that you realize how exquisite a physical art it is."
—**Christopher Morley,** *The Romany Stain*

"Cycling is necessarily a constant series of descents."
—**H. G. Wells,** *The Wheels of Chance*

"Now it is true that I could have learned without a teacher but it would have been risky for me."
—**Mark Twain,** "Taming the Bicycle"

"This is the first lesson of teaching your kids to be mountain bikers: There comes a day when the kid is better than you."
—**Mark Mozer**

"One large bruise on the shin is even more characteristic of the 'prentice cyclist, for upon every one of them waits the jest of the unexpected treadle. You try at least to walk your machine in an easy manner, and whack!—you are rubbing your shin."

—H. G. Wells, *The Wheels of Chance*

RIDING WITH STYLE

"A bike can be an important appurtenance of an important ritual. Moving the legs evenly and steadily soon brings home to the bike rider a valuable knowledge of pace and rhythm, and a sensible respect for timing and the meeting of a schedule. Out of rhythm come many things, perhaps all things."

—**William Saroyan,** *The Bicycle Rider in Beverly Hills*

When I teach mountain biking classes and skills clinics, sometimes I talk about the curse of competence—a mysterious lack of something that keeps average riders average. Competent riders have legs that can spin the pedals into a blur. Their lungs are bellows. Their hearts rumble with power. They are mighty machines, but they are merely machines. They do not ride with their heads. Or maybe their souls, as goofy or pretentious as that might sound.

I am a good rider. I am not a great rider but I have ridden with great riders. I have eaten with them and hung with them, interviewed them, and talked with them when there was no purpose except to talk. I have seen great riders make tiny movements on a bike that most people never notice, little tricks of the hands or feet, certain ways of sitting, a way of breathing. I have tried—and failed—to copy these tiny movements and translate them into my own greatness, and finally realized it is not the movements that matter but the thought behind them.

Cycling style counts, but only when it exists for a reason. Style as style is its own caricature, a cartoony costume for the competent rider hidden inside. Style that emanates from your own idea of how you want to ride—that is what mystics or mountain bikers might call the one true path. This kind of style will infuse and elevate everything you do on a bike, from the smallest things such as clicking into a pedal or how you hold your fingers on the handlebar to broader concepts such as knowing when to attack or how to play a race like a chess game.

Unfortunately, that's all I know about riding with style—I have no idea how to develop this hard-to-define but easy-to-spot something, except to do what good riders have always done to become great: Ride a lot, observe and listen to everything, but adopt and then adapt only the techniques and tactics that fit your vision. In other words: Use only the good stuff. Sounds wonderfully impossible, doesn't it? Race you to the grail.

"My biggest fear is that they will confuse me with another racer."
   —Claudio Chiappucci

"Moments of panache, where I make a bit of an exploit, even if it doesn't end in victory, are real important for me personally, and I need to make efforts like that once or twice a year. They're important moments, and every once in a while I think it's good to show what you're made of."
   —Jean-Francois Bernard

"Ride like water."
   —Paul Adkins

"The more it hurts, the farther ahead I'm getting."
   —Dave Fornes

"Mountain bike riding should not be based on a Judeo-Christian principle of sin and redemption, where you're overcoming and conquering or else paying for your failure to do so. Mountain biking should be a Buddhist relationship between you and the environment you're in, where

you're the environment and the environment is you and, free from conflict, riding becomes a means for personal expression."
   —Bob Roll

"You can't mountain bike and think about dinner or divorce or the bills. You need to be one big sensory receptor if you're going to stay within the margins of control. You need to be like an animal. They don't think about bills."
   —Jacquie Phelan

"Develop the ability to concentrate without the slightest letup when you race. If you can learn to concentrate that way, you can avoid a lot of mechanicals and injuries."
   —Charlie Cunningham

"If my mind wandered I might have slowed one second on every lap. That would have been twenty minutes over the 1,306 laps and would have cost me the record."
   —Michael White, on his 12-hour world record of
      270.621 miles

"If you're doing a thousand-kilometer event you don't think of it all at once because your mind just can't fathom it. What you do is you break it into achievable goals that you know you can do. If you're used to riding fifty kilometers then that's all you do is ride the first fifty kilometers. And you just keep adjusting that as the ride progresses, because there will be times where you're just thinking about the next telephone pole. Or the top of the next hill."

—Jeff Shmoorkoff

"When you're on the starting line of your first century, it's not wise to sit there and think, 'I've got to ride one hundred miles.' I remember my first one, and my thought was to get to the first rest stop. I made each succeeding rest stop my goal. When they're about twenty-five miles apart, you don't get intimidated by what seems an impossible distance. All you need to do is ride twenty-five miles four times."

—Seana Hogan

"I believe in pacing. I go as hard as I can, and whether I'm leading or not I'll keep the same pace. So far, this has been good enough."

—Juli Furtado

"They say if you don't crash you're not pushing your limits. But I don't like the feeling of being out of control. You try to find your edge. The controlled edge is a special feeling."

—Cindy Devine

"You have to learn how to channel and focus your energy. It builds up, and you need to be able to release it when the right time comes—not before your downhill run, or after it, but during the few minutes it's happening."

—Greg Herbold

"On the last lap I used to feel like I was being hunted from behind. I hated that, so I've changed to thinking about hunting the guys in front of me, no matter how bad I feel."

—Paul Willerton

⭐

"To really enjoy it, you have to take the worst stuff, the hardest stuff, the harshest stuff—and see it all as normal."

—Franck Roman, on mountain bike racing

"Fear is something you have to learn to control and use to your advantage because everyone has it. The difference is how you let it affect you. You have to be confident. If I'm at the top of the course and I notice a racer with fear in her eyes, I go up to her and say, 'Be strong and find the way of the peaceful warrior—you're gonna do great.'"
—**Missy Giove**

"Never use your face as a brake pad."
—**Jake Watson**

"There's no magic you'll be able to ride something in a race you can't in training."
—**Alison Sydor**

"Be satisfied with your preparation and try not to beat yourself up before you race. Whatever comes of it, at least you'll be getting a great training session."
—**Susan DeMattei**

"Learn to swear in different languages. Other riders will appreciate your efforts to communicate. They'll also know who you're talking to."

—**Robert Millar,** on fitting into a pro peloton

"Laurent [Fignon] showed me the path to follow, the discipline of respect, the art of consent."

—**Bjarne Riis**

"I learned a lot from Hinault. He was so strong, obviously the great rider of his era. But sometimes when I'd try to help him, we'd have communication problems. So he'd literally steer me around in the field. That was a great way to learn."

—**Andy Hampsten,** on riding with Bernard Hinault

"Train your weakness and race your strength."

—**Chris Carmichael**

"When riding, the mind should precede the rider by one bike length. Figuratively speaking."

—**William Nealy,** *Mountain Bike!*

"You want to ride like silk gliding on soft air. Think slow and smooth and one day you'll discover you're riding so easy you'll laugh out loud at the joy of it all. You'll also discover you're moving fast, probably faster than you ever imagined riding. Don't panic. The speed flowed out of the silk."

—Hank Barlow

"The more you can disconnect from mechanical and gravitational forces, the more you cease seeing trails as problems to be solved, and the more you will transcend the forces of gravity and mechanics. When you finally disconnect, the trail will look different. There will be no obstacles. You'll see it like a canvas or piece of paper on which you can express yourself."

—Bob Roll

✦

"I didn't have any typical teammates. There was no particular criteria. I refused to have any racers who were even rumored to be on drugs or steroids. I placed importance on spiritual and moral values. Those who are with me must possess an inner sense of the race, knowing when to fan out at the proper moment, when to control the escapes without my intervention. I hate to have to give orders."

—Eddy Merckx

"The spontaneous motivations and movements of packs and riders must be gauged intuitively. Observe the tempo of the pace, and the movement of the peloton, especially in the waning moments. A look into others' eyes reveals fatigue, which rarely can be disguised. These are only some of the variables that can betray the moment's secrets."

—Laurence Malone

"When I get in a race, I'm nobody's friend."

—Davis Phinney

"I decided I'd give him another ten seconds. Finally I said to myself, 'Here I go, follow me.' I mean, it was getting hot in the rubber suit. I was sweating all over the track."

—Nelson Vails, on his one-minute-plus trackstand against Philippe Vernet in the 1984 Olympics

"If you race just to try and make someone else lose, then what's the point? Even if you're in a break with a faster rider, it's still worth riding to win."

—Max Sciandri

"My advice to novices is this: Who needs to know about tactics, as long as he is not fit enough to dominate even his local events? Who believes that tactics come first and ability later is a fool. The only good tactics for youngsters are these: Train well, live clean, eat well (but not unwisely), go to bed early every night and in the race, attack, boy, attack!"

—Charles Ruys

"When Bernard Hinault was in New York years ago, a magazine editor asked him, 'what psychological psych-ups do you use before a race? Do you imagine the race or hear voices telling you to psych up?' Hinault rolled on the bed—I'm not kidding you—for twenty minutes just laughing."

—Greg LeMond

"As long as I breathe, I attack."

—Bernard Hinault

"A solo attack is just intuition, just feeling, nothing short of destiny that tells you to go for it."
—**Jacky Durand**

"Early attacks and breaks rarely succeed. It's after the halfway point that the race really begins."
—**Ron Kiefel**

"When you make a move, even if you realize it's the wrong move, go with it. I've lost races because I started a move then stopped. That's one of the things I've carried through my career."
—**Connie Young**

"Guitarist Larry Coryell once told me that the spaces between the notes are as important as the notes themselves. So it is with bike racing; the time between attacks is vital to appreciate the game."
—**John Derven**

"When you're doing a domestique's job, it's not very often that you have to think about your energy towards the end of the stage other than how you're going to come up for the next day. You get to the finish however you can, you get through the next day however you can. But in crucial moments that can be decisive you've got to give a hundred percent of what you've got on the given day, and the next day if I get shelled or lose half an hour it doesn't really matter when you know you helped make the key move."

—Neil Stephens

"I'm not even sure what pulse rate I normally use for a time trial. I just go on the feeling in my legs."

—Ivan Gotti

"The saddle is the hand of god: It can push you up hills or throw you to the ground."

—John Olsen

"Shifting is done as much with the eyes as with the hands. Most people don't anticipate."

—Tom Hillard

"In the city, ride like you're invisible. As if nobody can see you. Because a huge percentage of the time, nobody can."
   —Jason Makapagal

"The objective for any domestique is to go in and try to do the best you can to help the team. You've either got to win or you've got to work."
   —Neil Stephens

★

"I tried to put them on the ground, and the next time I'll use my fist instead."
   —Roberto Visentini, on why he swerved into his teammates Stephen Roche and Eddy Schepers during the 1987 Giro, in which he and Roche battled for the victory

DESIRE

"I finally concluded that all failure was from a wobbling will rather than a wobbling wheel."

 —**Frances Willard,** *How I Learned to Ride the Bicycle*

Desire is one of the things that make great riders great. But not even the world's best cyclist has any more desire than the rest of us. God, or genetics, or the chemistry of creation —or whatever you pray to or put under an electron microscope—does not parcel out unequal and unchangeable amounts of qualities such as love or cynicism, the will to win or the urge to ride better than you're supposed to be able to.

Every person who's spun a single pedal stroke has felt some flicker of obsession. It's just that certain riders are able to access that feeling easier than the rest of us. Ned Overend's desire is no more passionate or deeper than yours or mine. He's just spent so much time chasing his desire that he knows where to find it, and when he finds it he can draw more from it. Desire fulfills itself, a kind of perpetual-motion emotion that produces more and more as more and more is used, until eventually the stuff just pours out of some people.

So although not everyone can be a great rider, anyone can have a great ride. I believe that. But sometimes during dark days when I ride no better than I did ten years ago, when I watch my friends drift away on some current I can't catch, I wonder if the theory of infinite desire is just a way to feel better about being so ordinary. Worse than a rationalization: an apology to myself. Then I remember the flower race.

My wife and I eloped to Block Island, a tiny speck of earth floating just off the Atlantic coast. Cars weren't allowed on the ferry so we took two mountain bikes, lugging our bags slung across our backs but somehow happier for the burden. Just like it should be but almost never is, our marriage day was the best of our lives. It rained the Sunday we were supposed to leave, so we stashed our bags in the hotel van and Beth drove with them to the ferry dock. Our muddy bikes weren't allowed in the van, so I rode one bike and balanced the other beside me.

The last ferry left at 4:30. I finished the two-mile ride at 4:15, and Beth walked up to me and said, "I forgot my flowers."

I dropped her bike and sprinted away. We were poor. We'd spent twenty-five dollars on a bouquet of wildflowers, living vines, and grasses. I'd spent most of my life riding and racing, getting fitter and faster every year, but for what? I'd won some money, a few T-shirts, bragging rights and a little pride. Suddenly I found myself in the race of my life, chasing a cheap flower arrangement that had more value than all the prizes in the world.

I didn't win the flower race. Desire did, sliding through wet turns and hopping curbs with a deep and powerful determination as great as anyone has ever ridden with.

"There are lots of very fit and skilled people out there—people who are pretty much equal to each other—but there's always going to be one who's going to win more than the others. I don't know how to explain mental toughness, or killer instinct, or knowing how to win."

—Juli Furtado

"I'm on the bike and I go into a rage—I shriek for about five seconds, I shake like mad, my eyes kind of bulge, and I'd never quit. That's heart. That's soul. That's guts."

—Lance Armstrong

"I ride for passion. Cycling is too hard to do just for the money."

—Paola Pezzo

"I'm not a normal cyclist, I have nothing in common with the guys who just ride their bikes. There aren't many riders who have the same passion as me."

—Richard Virenque

"Bike racing is art. Art is driven by passion, by emotions, by unknown thoughts. The blood that pumps through my veins is stirred by emotion. It's the same for every athlete. And that's why we do this."

—Chris Carmichael

"I like extreme, intense situations. The more extreme the better. If there's a thunderstorm during a race, it's great. I'm great."

—Missy Giove

"My doctor said that I'm lucky to be alive and breathing. I told him that my house plants are alive and breathing. I'm only happy when I'm on two wheels and going 60 mph."

—Dave Cullinan, recovering from open-heart surgery and a heart attack at age 24

"If you're going to be a world champion, you have to be your own hero."

—Travis Brown

"I lost the lead to a French rider when my chain skipped. Then as we rode through the feed zone the French coach told her that she could beat me on the downhill section. What she didn't know was that I speak French. It got me mad, and I passed her back."

—Lisa Lamoreaux, on winning the veteran cross-country world championship in 1994

"At some point I figured out that it's all about fun. If you bang your head against a wall and scream, 'I wanna win,' it won't happen. Have passion."

—Myles Rockwell

"Attacking is something that was born in me. Something I like."

—Peter Luttenberger

"I just broke my shoulder, so I'm only going to race the downhill."

    —**Marla Streb,** explaining why she wouldn't compete in both the cross-country and downhill races at the Vail World Championships in 1994

"They should not have too many Romingers. That kind of guy gives the impression that he is just out there doing his job. For me, it is a passion. When I stop, I will be proud to have served and glorified the sport of bicycle racing."

    —**Claudio Chiappucci,** on the styles of Tony Rominger and himself

"We each carry our own Tour de France inside us."

    —**Philippe Brunel,** *An Intimate Portrait of the Tour de France*

"I used to do a lot of mental callousing. It took me a long time to feel that pain is good."

    —**John Stamstad**

"On a given race day, I can summon whatever physical ability I have on that day. I'm usually spent after a race. What I'm saying is, you may be talented, but you may not be prepared to suffer."

—**Ned Overend**

"When you want to do something you give yourself up to it completely, and someone who doesn't want to do it as much won't go as well because they will feel the pain more."

—**Richard Virenque**

"I have to really believe that I can medal, and then I'll do whatever it takes every day to prepare myself for when that time comes. If I don't think I can, then I'm not going to give it that hundred percent or more that I need to give, to suffer. You have to find that line and go just beyond it."

—**Tinker Juarez**

"Only a few times in his life, perhaps never, does a rider push himself to the absolute limit, or ten-tenths as I call it. Most of the time you ride pretty close to it, say at about eight-tenths. Nine is really suffering. But ten is how you'd ride if to be caught meant disembowelment or the torture of the hooks, or to save your mother or your children. It means to ride so that parts you never think of, such as your liver, your whole system, refuse to do any more. I've seen men try it. Sometimes they succeed, but mostly they finish in the ambulance. Usually they faint and crash at about nine-and-a-half tenths."

—**Ralph Hurne,** *The Yellow Jersey*

"You've got to be willing to rip it all apart, including yourself."

—**Steve Woznik**

"Cipollini is a rider who wants to do his work well, and remain at a high level, taking advantage of his physical ability. The rest is meaningless."

—**Mario Cipollini**

"There are three ways to pedal a bike. With the legs, with the lungs, or with the heart."

—**Mandible Jones,** "Carpet Particles"

"Fabio died, but you can have other accidents when you could be disabled or severely injured, which would take away your career. It's on my mind when I race, in a positive sense, if you can say that. It doesn't change your attitude to risk, but maybe motivates you to seize the day because you don't know what will happen the next day, and Fabio doesn't have a chance to."

  —**Lance Armstrong,** the day of the death of his
      teammate Fabio Casartelli during the 1995
      Tour de France

"Today, I rode with the strength of two men."

  —**Lance Armstrong,** after winning a Tour de France
      stage to honor Fabio Casartelli two days after
      his death

"Dairy Queen. God, I dream about Dairy Queens."

  —**Greg LeMond,** when asked what he thinks about
      during races in Europe

"I don't fail to finish because I'm physically not up to it, but because I get mentally tired."

  —**Mario Cipollini**

"The real race is not on the hot, paved roads, the torturous off-road course or the smooth-surfaced velodrome. It is in the electrochemical pathways of your mind."
—**Alexi Grewal**

"Your mind will burn out before your body. Your body can adapt to almost anything. But there are people so crazy for cycling that they'll fry themselves."
—**Greg LeMond**

"I never raced to break records. I raced to enjoy myself."
—**Bernard Hinault**

"Bernard enjoyed hurting people, riding them into the ground."
—**Steve Bauer**

"If a rider has true talent, and has proved that he is really good, then he can be good again."
—**Gerrie Knetemann**

"Some people are not in control of their cycling. The cycling is in control of them. You get to a point where you say, 'Oh my God, I'm a motor for my bicycle. I'm no longer a person.'"
　—Rich Stark

"When it comes time to say go, your personality has to change. To some extent you've got to turn into a jerk. You have to have a little hate in your heart to want to stomp the competition."
　—Bob Gregario

"In 1990, every race I told myself you have to win, you have to win, you have to win. In this state you make mistakes."
　—Jean-Paul Van Poppel

"You go very strong, but you are too often resigned to be second. You have to be more audacious, more ambitious."
　—Maurice de Muer, to two-time Tour de France
winner Bernard Thevenet

"Me, I never dreamed of becoming a star—never! If it wasn't that I am gifted in cycling, I would not have persevered in the sport."
   —Miguel Indurain

"I've had a few results in my career, I suppose, and I'm quite proud of them, but I'm probably more proud of the work I've done as a domestique. I think I prefer that to having the responsibility of winning for myself."
   —Neil Stephens

"I don't want to die riding a bicycle. I prefer to give up."
   —Jacques Anquetil

"Anquetil took pleasure in provoking destiny."
   —Philippe Brunel, *An Intimate Portrait of the Tour de France*

"I would do it all over again, and even better."
   —Eddy Merckx, asked a silly question

THE TOUR DE FRANCE AND OTHER GREAT RACES

"I have started many stories about bicycle racing but have never written one that is as good as the races are both on the indoor and outdoor tracks and on the roads."
—**Ernest Hemingway,** *A Moveable Feast*

THE TOUR DE FRANCE AND
OTHER GREAT RACES

You dream of the Tour. You dream of the Tour de France when you sleep and when you hurt on a ride. You dream of the Tour sometimes when you see a bike, a racing bike streaking its silhouette down a darkening street, or sometimes just when you see a clunky city bike leaning against a brick wall. You do not know why this reminds you of the Tour, but all things bicycle do.

Sometimes in the dream you are riding the Tour. Sometimes you are just watching it pass, you are just one of those people rising from a checkered picnic blanket spread over a golden field outside of a town that seems make-believe to you. In your excitement you have spilled your wine and still hold a baguette end in one hand. A lone rider passes first, a solitary racer arched over his bike in concentration but who still looks over and smiles—you will swear later when you tell the story that he smiles—when he hears your cheers. Then a quick little knot of blurry color, the chase group intent and dangerous. Then the long whoosh of the peloton, the human train of noise and chatter that has created its own wind, that sweeps by quicker than it seems something that long should. Then the stragglers, the laughing group who make eye contact and wave to you, but by then you are sitting down again eating, your mouth too full to shout encouragement.

Or you are on a mountain. You have walked the mountain because the road was choked with cars and ready to close anyway. You have walked seven switchbacks and now you are at the front of a wall of people and the blaring cars and throaty motorcycles and the carnival of the lead vehicles has passed and you are leaning over to see two riders taunt each other up the mountain. When they get close you will lean farther over and scream into their faces, and you will try to run a little way beside them, and you will look into their eyes and you will never forget what you see there, ever, not as long as you can remember anything.

Sometimes the dream is not the Tour. Sometimes it is Paris-Roubaix. Sometimes you shred France's legendary Cap d'Ail or Mt. Ventoux descents, sometimes you are a blur on Mammoth Mountain or a cross-country racer flowing like water down Mt. Snow's slimy singletracks. When you dream of these races, you ride.

Sometimes you ride the Tour in your dreams, but it seems funny to you how often you do not. When you do ride it, you never win. You ride a fantastic climb, or run down an uncatchable break for your team, but you do not win and that seems right. Not even in a dream.

"This is the war of cyclists. That's what we call it."
    —Pedro Delgado, on the Tour de France

"There is no room in the Tour for the sick or the weak."
    —Laurent Jalabert

"It's a crucifixion, and the way to the cross has fourteen stations."
    —Henri Pelissier, on the Tour de France

"When you're a kid eighteen years old, seventeen, all you dream is to win the Tour de France. There are a lot of seventeen-year-olds out there doing it, but I tell you it's more difficult than people think. If I'd known how hard it was, my dreams at seventeen would have changed."
    —Greg LeMond

"The whole world has become much more interested in security. There is so much misery in this world that everybody looks for peace and quiet. The Tour de France refuses security. It involves and needs the concept of facing pain and defeat. Sacrifice is partly responsible for the Tour's popularity. Sacrifice is part of cycling's legend, certainly part of the Tour's legend."

—Jacques Goddet

"Everyday we take risks. People throw dirt and stones at us, they try to put branches between our spokes, going further would be like heading into a slaughterhouse."

—Gino Bartali, on abandoning the 1950 Tour de France

"Every top rider has had a terrible Tour de France. Indurain quit. Delgado quit. Even Merckx quit. You can't judge cyclists by one Tour."

—Greg LeMond

"A rider has to go to his limits and beyond to win such a tour as the Giro, and then finds himself able to go even further in the Tour de France."

—Jacques Anquetil

"First week you feel good, the second week you lose strength. Third week, fucked."
　　—**Per Pedersen,** on the Tour de France

"It's a love/hate relationship, and it's not until you come back that you remember how much you hate it."
　　—**Sean Yates,** on the Tour de France

"Every minute of every day of the Tour de France was hard. There were always attacks going, which made it really nerve-wracking. One week I slept just ten hours because I was so exhausted I couldn't sleep. I just lay in bed. Every nerve ending felt like it was exposed to rushing wind. You can't tell anyone how hard it is. You can't represent the suffering."
　　—**Bob Roll**

"Cycling is such a long endurance sport in terms of hours but it's also such a tactical sport that there are times when you could be just strolling along. But it can also be very intense, like a 3,000-meter run. The Tour de France is the one event where you combine all those intensity levels together for three weeks straight."
　　—**Greg LeMond**

"The Tour lasts twenty-one days and riders like me sometimes ask ourselves if it's worth all the effort for one stage win. It is."
—**Pascal Richard**

"Right now, I would sign an agreement to win the Tour and spend the rest of the season coming second. It's the best race in the world."
—**Miguel Indurain**

"Rightly or wrongly, riders are judged by how they do in the Tour de France."
—**Greg LeMond**

"In every Tour, we see the winners of future Tours."
—**Pierre Chany**

"Great riders don't make the Tour. The Tour makes great riders."
—**Ralph Hurne,** *The Yellow Jersey*

"The average American will never fully understand the Tour. It is the equivalent of the Super Bowl, but every day for twenty-three days. With up to a million spectators on the roadside and countless millions watching on TV, I doubt there is any sporting equivalent to compare it to."
   —**Phil Liggett**

"In the old days, Hugo Koblet chased after women as avidly as he went after the day's yellow jersey, Gino Bartali smoked cigarettes under his coach Coppi's nose and Jacques Anquetil rarely went anywhere without Janine, his platinum blonde 'Dame Blanche.' Champions mixed their private life with that of the Tour de France without fear of exposure, and the close quarters injected a heady dose of romanticism into the story of the race."
   —**Philippe Brunel,** *An Intimate Portrait of the Tour de France*

"The sport of cycling changed my life. Everything I do is based on the passion I learned from the Tour de France."
   —**John Tesh**

"I'm proud of what I've done in the Tour, but you have to keep your perspective. It's just a bicycle race after all."

—**Miguel Indurain,** after his fourth Tour de France win

"The problem with being a Tour de France winner is you always have that feeling of disappointment if you don't win again. That's the curse of the Tour de France."

—**Greg LeMond**

"I don't know too many people who even finish pro road classics. It's seven hours of racing. The pace goes from 30 kph to 60 kph, then back to 30 and up to 60 again. You're fighting with the peloton the entire way."

—**Alexi Grewal**

"To grind out a win in one of the long, one-day Spring Classics, you've got to want to inflict pain. Ever read how people say it's really personal when you stab someone? Well, a Classic is that kind of personal. There's nothing neat or clinical about it. There's no divorcing the passion and emotion from the act. It's visceral."

—**Chris Carmichael**

"Paris-Roubaix is a pile of shit. You're up to your neck in mud and you're riding in mud and you don't have time to piss. It's a pile of shit. It's the most wonderful race in the world."
—**Teho de Rooy**

"In my living room there are no photographs from my career but there is a big cobblestone. It's the trophy they give to the winner of Paris-Roubaix. And every morning when I wake up, that big cobblestone looks at me."
—**Hennie Kuiper**

"In the Tour of Italy there are two races: race to be first overall and race to be first Italian."
—**Stephen Roche**

"Merckx rivaled the true climbers in the mountains. He feared no sprinter beyond 200 meters. Able to dominate the stopwatch, he felt no pain against cold or heat, a fact he amply demonstrated in the famous Trois Cimes de Lavarado [1968 Giro] which showed ghostly racers lost in the snow, between the snowdrifts, some hiding under thick blankets mad as hell, others holding on like mad to the doors of cars that were trying to light their way on the

road, and yet others, the most clever, inside the cars thinking they could fool the eye of the race commissioner."
—**Philippe Brunel,** *An Intimate Portrait of the Tour de France*

"The behavior of the fans was bad. As well as the punching and pushing, they were spitting wine at me. There was also some kind of grain that they were spitting at me. At the finish I was really dirty from the stuff they had spat at me."
—**Stephen Roche,** on the 1987 Giro he won over his Italian teammate

"The hour record is everything."
—**Graeme Obree**

"Throughout this hour, the longest of my career, I never knew a moment of weakness, but the effort was never easy. It's not possible to compare the hour with a time trial on the road. Here it's not possible to ease up, to change gears or the rhythm. The hour record demands a total effort, permanent and intense. I will never try it again."
—**Eddy Merckx,** after setting the hour record at 49.431 kilometers

"Everyone told me this would be the most excruciating effort I've ever made, but frankly it wasn't."

 —**Tony Rominger,** after setting the hour record at
  53.832 kilometers

"Basically, I just accepted that this would be the hardest thing I'd ever done, and when I'd done it, I'd never want to do it again. Then, when it started, it didn't actually hurt that much. I could not have gone any faster, but it didn't hurt."

 —**Chris Boardman,** after setting the hour record at
  56.375 kilometers

"When we got into New York, the darkness was turning to light, and Lon Haldeman was approaching the George Washington Bridge. This was the most spectacularly clear day I'd ever seen in New York City, and from the bridge you could look straight down the island and see the Empire State Building sticking out against the horizon as though it had been painted there. And that Lon was so exhausted riding along the bridge that he looked straight forward the whole time and never once turned his head the three inches to the right to see the Empire State Building just affected me so deeply that I was crying."

> —**Jim Lampley,** in 1982 covering the first cross-country Great American Bike Race, which later became the Race Across America

"At one point, I looked down at my legs and through a layer of ice and grease, I could see that they were bright red. After that, I didn't look at my legs again."

> —**Andy Hampsten,** on his legendary rain- and snow-plagued ride up the Gavia Pass in the '88 Giro

"You spend your whole year doing nothing but training for this race, and then you get one shot. You feel you have to win because if you don't the year is garbage."

> —**Rob Kish,** on RAAM

"Nine or ten days of continuous cycling leave a lot of time for introspection. I think it's the learning about myself that brings me back to cross-country races."

> —**Lon Haldeman,** on RAAM

"The Tour is about humans conquering the obstacles of the world. There's nothing special about being able to ride a bike or climb a mountain, but the way the Tour riders do it . . ."

—Phil Liggett

"Just as the one-day world championships are not as reflective of overall talent as the World Cup series, neither are the Olympics anywhere close to crowning the best riders in the world. But the rainbow jersey carries more prestige than three Grundig champion jerseys, and Olympic gold reflects something greater than anything the sport can provide in its more honest and authentic events."

—Zapata Espinoza

"I went home, went on some easy training rides, and reflected on my cycling career. That's when I decided— Hey, I'd like to win the world championship on my birthday."

—Johan Museeuw, after his 1996 rainbow jersey victory

"Anything could happen during a 6-day race. Riders were jerked from their cots and rode through jams on the track, then returned to sleep with no memory of having been awakened. They were like soldiers in the World War who fell asleep while marching."

    —**Alf Goullet,** quoted in *The Saturday Evening Post,* 1926

"This race is going to be great. It has everything—ice, snow, dirt roads, no air."

    —**Dave Pelletier,** on the 14,100-foot Pikes Peak hillclimb at the 1986 world championships

LEGENDS, MYTHS
AND CHAMPIONS

"God wishes he was Eddy Merckx."
—Punchline to a cycling joke*

LEGENDS, MYTHS AND CHAMPIONS

We are forgetting how to write and talk about cycling. Our race stories are blow-by-blow accounts, analysis and second-guessing. Even among ourselves, relating a race to friends over beers, we have begun communicating like television broadcasters: citing statistics, numbers and facts to give ourselves credibility, aiming for the clever quip, explaining the importance of the latest equipment and technology, focusing on top-secret training and nutrition programs, duly crediting the scientific edge.

We think we know more now about cycling than ever—and maybe we do—but if we're not careful our sophistication will cost us our legends. We will lose our legends as we dilute our own ability to exalt cyclists, to cheer as the great ones climb onto pedestals and wail as others refuse to leave the same ground we mortals occupy.

My all-time favorite cycling writer is an old French guy named Philippe Brunel. He writes about cycling as if he's standing by Homer's side, scribbling accounts of the epics he sees. About Eddy Merckx, he wrote that, "This dictator was an angel. This sphinx was an ecumenical and taciturn human being that destiny refused to spare." And of Claudio Chiappucci's risk-taking: "It's what made him sublime or pathetic, nothing in between. He incarnated a new kind of hero."

Another writer we should listen to, Antoine Blondin, once reported that the great but eternally unlucky Raymond Poulidor "wore his malediction like a virtual coat of shining armor."

Cycling is so childlike in so many ways, in so many of the feelings and emotions it gives us—the fresh feel of escape, the catch in your throat at the start of a descent, the controlled fear you sometimes summon just to enjoy, the simple sensation of being alive and realizing it. Children have heroes. Unlike adults, they aren't embarrassed by reverence. Listen to what your bike is telling you about cycling. Watch a race with it, with your hand resting on the top tube. Listen to your bike narrate the heroics, and then tell someone else what you heard.

"Fans kissed Gino Bartali's bike. Babies were held out for his blessing. Followers swept the dusty road before him with their jackets to lessen the risk of puncture. At night, during a major race, fans would call for him so persistently that he was forced to use ear plugs."
—Ralph Hurne

"From snowstorm, water, ice, Bartali arose majestically like an angel covered with mud, wearing under his soaked tunic the precious soul of an exceptional champion."
—Jacques Goddet, in his Tour de France notes on Bartali's 1948 victory

"Bartali belongs to those who accept the dogma. He is metaphysical. He is protected by the saints."
—Culzio Malaparte

"Do not touch—he is a god."
—Sports Minister General Antonelli, trying to disperse the crowd after Gino Bartali won the 1937 Tour de France

"Bartali's secret was a slow heart; it used to thump about once every hour and when it did it gave him enough strength to ride up the side of the Eiffel Tower."
—**Ralph Hurne,** *The Yellow Jersey*

"In Coppi's veins gas flows, but in Bartali only blood flows."
—**Dino Buzzati**

"Coppi? Is that the one we followed in the Giro del Piemonte? The guy who is as skinny as an asparagus? He doesn't lack courage, I'll give him that, but I think he's kind of fragile."
—**Gino Bartali,** on his first impression of rival
    Fausto Coppi

"I have won Paris-Roubaix!"
"And Coppi?"—who finished first—asked journalists.
"Oh; he was untouchable! I consider that I actually won."
—**Maurice Diot,** on finishing second to Fausto
    Coppi in the 1950 Paris-Roubaix

"I was in top gear and flying over the cobbles, cutting every corner. [Fausto] Coppi gave me the blackest look and then accelerated. I was riding in a black tunnel just focusing on Coppi's wheel. Every time he looked back I tried to appear indifferent, but I don't think I was very convincing. Over and over Fausto accelerated. They weren't explosive jumps, more like fast increases in the tempo until everything was screaming inside me. Then I noticed that he wasn't going so fast, that even he, Fausto Coppi, had human limits."
   —Rik Van Steenbergen

"On the outside, Merckx appeared calm but inside he hid a tormented and worried soul. In the middle of the night before a big classic, he would awaken to heighten his bicycle seat a millimeter or correct the inclination of his handlebar before returning to bed totally appeased. This dictator was an angel. This sphinx was an ecumenical and taciturn human being that destiny refused to spare."
   —Philippe Brunel, *An Intimate Portrait of the Tour de France*

"You can have the same rider as Eddy Merckx, with the same force, the same ability and things like that but you will never have a guy who will win so many races. Merckx started on the first day of January in six-day races, two weeks later he made a cyclocross and then he started his preparation for the road season. He was on the top level for twelve months of the year."

—**Harry van den Bremt**

"It is possible that Fausto Coppi had dominated Merckx on certain days in the mountain climbs, and we can reasonably think that Jacques Anquetil could have beaten him against the stopwatch, but there was in Merckx a little of both men, plus something indefinable, like a soul supplement. To that thought, Merckx was Coppi, plus Anquetil and Van Looy. He was, in short, the incarnation of bravery itself."

—**Philippe Brunel,** *An Intimate Portrait of the Tour de France*

"On the continent of Europe it is said that 21 July 1969 was an important day in world history. For two reasons. A man called Neil Armstrong walked on the moon and a man called Eddy Merckx won his first Tour de France."

—**David Walsh,** *The Agony and the Ecstasy*

"Other champions will come to take the place of Miguel Indurain, the product of a standardized society, team leader of programmed cycling. We will live with other grand Tours, other emotions in the same order, but one question will persist, begging to be answered. That question is: Who will do better than Merckx?"

—**Philippe Brunel,** *An Intimate Portrait of the Tour de France*

"I hold in my hand a born cyclist, whose actions make me think of the movements of a clock."

—**Andre Boucher,** on first seeing Jacques Anquetil

"Hinault wanted to be stronger than any human being, stronger than the events and those feelings which had made him at times very arrogant. Beyond that, he was like any other man."

—**Philippe Brunel,** *An Intimate Portrait of the Tour de France*

"Do your homework, because you'll never make money riding a bike."

—**Greg LeMond's** high-school history teacher

"LeMond was a study in perfect riding posture and bike fit. He did not fight the bicycle."
  —Edmund Burke

"LeMond was in trouble. He had a bout of diarrhea. He rode by me with thirty kilometers to go, surrounded by his domestiques bringing him to the front. God, the smell was terrible. It was rolling down his legs. I know if it was me I would stop. But then I am not capable of winning the Tour de France. He is, and I suppose that's the difference."
  —Paul Kimmage

"I've only known one other rider able to dominate the way Indurain does, and that was Eddy Merckx. But Merckx was a robot and his force humiliated his opponents. Miguel is a lord. He's generous and he respects his opponents."
  —Jose Echavarri, on Miguel Indurain

"The lads are afraid to ride behind Miguel. His turns at the front are too long and too hard and they finish totally exhausted."
  —Gerard Rue, on riding the team time trial with
      Miguel Indurain

"Miguel is a slow person. Miguel Indurain took time learning to become a man, because in him everything had to be connected. He had to be sure of his strength and balance before he could show his talent in full force."
   —Jose Echavarri

"Indurain's a bit like a lizard . . . he thrives only in the hotter climates."
   —Phil Liggett

"I always dreamed of making Miguel a champion, but above all I wanted to make him a man. Like Anquetil, who was a fabulous man, whose philosophy was 'live and let live.' You have to think of yourself but you should never humiliate others. It pleases me very much when people compare Miguel and Anquetil."
   —Jose Echavarri

"Miguel Indurain is from another planet."
   —Gianni Bugno

"David Tinker Juarez is some amazing angel walking amongst us. Tinker is beautiful. As a matter of fact, Tinker is absolutely gorgeous. I love Tinker not necessarily to look at, but rather to observe. Since I come from a long, often oppressive career as a road pro in Europe, seeing someone so raw, so unencumbered by convention—it's brought a lot of joy to my severely jaded heart."

—Bob Roll

"A popular rumor was that for training he would go out on epic rides wearing a backpack filled with rocks. Such is the legend of Tinker."

—Zapata Espinoza

"I think Thomas Frischknecht is the greatest cross-country racer in the world."

—Ned Overend

"I first saw Ned in Malibu at the Outlaw race when he won the hillclimb. He sat down, took off his helmet, and was sunning himself when the guy in second finally got there. Ned is an inspiration for all of us—he is a freak of nature."

—John Parker, on Ned Overend

"My first race with him was in 1986, and my biggest impression as a kid was looking at his calves, you know 'cause his calves are sooooo ripped. Whenever I got dropped by him, I always ended up looking at his calves. As I slowly got dropped, I'd think, 'Shit, I gotta get calves like that.' But I never did."

—**Rishi Grewal,** on Ned Overend

"Hans views the world as one big trials obstacle."

—**Bob Allen,** on trials champion Hans Rey

"Hans doesn't ride like a nervous bunny on a pogo stick like many trials riders. He rides like a leopard: smooth and aggressive."

—**John Olsen**

"Most people's standards are set by who they race against, but not George Mount. George is one of those break-through guys who said, 'I'm in this race but I'm not racing against you. My head is in another planet.'"

—**Owen Mulholland**

"As for Juli, she's on her own planet. Sometimes people are just at the right place at the right time doing what they are meant to do in life—like Michael Jordan playing basketball. That's Juli."

—Doug Martin, on Juli Furtado

"She can put one minute on the field on a climb, and gain another on the descent. She can descend better than anyone."

—Daryl Price, on Juli Furtado

"Tomac looks a lot faster because he is fighting his bike."

—Thomas Frischknecht

"Lance is one in a million. Maybe one in ten million. The amount of fatigue-causing lactic acid produced by his cycling muscles is only one-fourth that of his competitors. There are few people with his ability walking the face of the earth."

—Edward Coyle, on Lance Armstrong

"Since he first showed himself in the Tour, facing Greg LeMond in 1990, he rarely came out the winner of a big battle, but he continued to be the cause of numerous skirmishes as fantasy faced reality. Unless under exceptional circumstances, the Carrera team leader will never win the Giro, nor the Tour, but he exists beyond those results. He lives where time has been charged with imposing his image on the public."

—**Claudio Gregario,** journalist, on Claudio Chiappucci

"Chiappucci raced for glory, and was unique in that account. He took risks and the public loved him for it. It's what made him sublime or pathetic, nothing in between. He incarnated a new kind of hero."

—**Philippe Brunel,** *An Intimate Portrait of the Tour de France*

"He's the Bartali of the poor. He may be less spiritual than the Gino of old, but he is just as much wedded to his job, and like Gino, he belongs to the people."

—**Dino Zandegu,** on Claudio Chiappucci

"If Keetie van Oosten-Hage's forward-on-the-saddle, nose-on-the-stem, elbows-at-90-degrees swaying style is less than the epitome of graceful elegance, then so much for graceful elegance. Her style answers the most fundamental demand: speed."
—Owen Mulholland

"Raymond Poulidor wore his malediction like a virtual coat of shining armor."
—Antoine Blondin

"Poulidor represents the soul of the French. Not someone totally committed to winning, but more or less someone who takes his time, who lives his life, who does it his own way. Someone who knows how to live."
—Kent

"Riis is a real champion who has gone out and sought victory at the hardest times of the race."
—Bernard Hinault

"His long face appears like the blade of a knife as he climbs without apparent effort."
—**Newspaper description** of Fausto Coppi

"Hinault—is he a superman or a fool?"
—**Phil Liggett,** as Bernard Hinault attacked in the mountains even though he had a five-minute lead in the '86 Tour de France

"Sean Yates was good enough but not selfish enough to be a top rider. The last of the great equipiers [team riders]."
—**Stephen Roche**

"Everyone thinks I'm the Dennis Rodman of mountain biking. I'm not like that at all—I'm really more like Blanche DuBois."
—**Bob Roll**

"At the top of his career, Gianni was afraid to sleep in his champion's clothes for fear he would wake up in the skin of a support rider."

—**Maria Fossati,** on Gianni Motta, a brilliant Italian rider of the 60s and 70s who never fulfilled his promise and quit cycling after winning the first stage of the Giro d'Italia in 1974

"Bottecchia has the look of a country boy, but in cycling . . . what style! He has arms and legs that never stop. I doubt anyone has taught him anything useful, but for sure he looks good on a bicycle. All of him is made for cycling."
—**Henri Pelissier**

"Stephen Roche filled me with wonder. There was something in the way he carried himself: a class, a magnificence. The one who came closest to Jacques Anquetil. Stephen believed it was his destiny to be a champion."
—**Raphael Geminiani**

"Stephen [Roche] was born with the ability to turn the pedals. You cannot teach yourself to do it the way he does."
—**Roger Legeay**

"Van Looy always had a perfumed handkerchief in his jersey back pocket. He need only to breathe in the scent of it and traces would waft back to us as his way of letting us know he was in front."

—**Unidentified pro** on Rik Van Looy

"When I won the [world championship] jersey it was a surprise. I took it and I wore it for a year and you don't realize at a young age, at a young point in your career, what you have. Then when you lose the jersey, you see another person wearing it, you realize exactly what it was that you achieved. It means more now."

—**Lance Armstrong**

"It's amazing how plain it is. It's just a regular Italian wool jersey with stripes across it. You look at it and say, 'That's sort of neat.' And my friends go, 'Whoa, man, that thing's way more than neat.'"

—**Greg Herbold,** on his world championship jersey

"As a champion you have to represent yourself well and your team and your sponsor well, but with the rainbow jersey you're also representing the sport and the jersey

itself. With that comes added pressure tenfold."
—**Lance Armstrong**

"When I first met Lance in 1992, he was so strong he could rip the cranks off the bike. Lance is Lance. There's absolutely nobody else in the world like him. He's not like the rest of us."
—**Frankie Andreau**

"To be a champion you need firstly, before anything, the physical capabilities, which come from birth. Then it's vital to have a strong character or courage. Finally, you must have the ambition to always push yourself."
—**Eddy Merckx**

"The rainbow jersey—it's so much harder to race with that. Even if you're bad in that jersey, they're going to follow your every move. Say if some guy won the championship on a fluke—took off on the gun and got 30 minutes and held them off—and was an undeserving world champion, everybody knew he was terrible, the next year when he was in the jersey they would still follow him around. Every move. Because of that jersey."
—**Lance Armstrong**

* So these three cyclists go out for a late-fall training ride. They're hammering along when suddenly they hit a spot of black ice and fly off a cliff. When the first cyclist opens his eyes, an angel is standing before him.

"Who do you wish to be?" asks the angel.

"Huh?" says the cyclist.

"Look, you rode well and lived well. When you get to heaven you can choose to transform yourself into any rider who ever lived."

Just then a racer in wool shorts and short-sleeved jersey whooshes by on a green bike. "Hey!" says the cyclist. "That's—"

"One of your friends," says the angel, "He chose to be Fausto Coppi. So who do you wish to be?"

At that moment The Cannibal rips by them. "Aww man," says the cyclist. "My other friend already took Eddy, didn't he?"

"Oh, no," says the angel. "Your other friend lived. That's just God. He wishes he was Eddy Merckx."

PAID TO PEDAL

"There's money in pro cycling if you're a star, a super champion. But for the average pro there's not much, and the unfairness of it all is that the difference between the stars and the rest is so slight. It can be the thickness of a tire, or a second or a minute, or six wins out of twelve instead of nine out of twelve. In my day I've beaten all the big names in cycling. Perhaps I've only done it the once or twice and they've screwed me more times than I've taken them, but I was never far behind, only the few yards that make the difference."

—**Ralph Hurne**, *The Yellow Jersey*

Think of all the jobs you've ever had, some job you stayed too long in. Think of all the mornings you did not want to get up because you did not want to start the job. Think of how the job ate into your life, how you dreamed of better occupations. Can cycling—this glorious act of spinning our feet around and rolling over the earth— really feel like that?

Yes. And no. Every pro I've met—whether that's racer, mechanic, messenger or coach—all talk of one day waking up and realizing that what they once did for love they now do for love and money. Or, sometimes, just money. They can tell you how it feels to enter races half a world from home when all you want is to see your home so you can remember what it looks like. To be ordered to attack when all you want to do is fall to the ground and close your eyes. To ride harder than most people ever ride, every day. To hammer through mud and cold rain, sick, getting sicker, but unable to stop.

But these are privileged complications—the complaints of gods—and the pros know that. The good ones, anyway. They know they live magic lives, and even when they won't admit it you can see it in how they carry themselves. You can see it in how they regard the rest of the world.

The world is the place they'll go when their luck runs out.

There's something else amazing about the average, ordinary, work-a-day bike rider: The worst pro in the world is a fantastic cyclist. The riders we give no chance of winning a race are exquisite bike handlers and hammers unlike any we have ever ridden with. That menacing messenger you cursed for running a red light then turning against traffic was riding a no-brakes, fixed-gear bike down the busiest street of one of the world's busiest cities. The mechanic with greased hands and no home except in a box van or on his brother-in-law's couch can fold himself out of a car window, stretch across a rotating wheel and adjust a jittery derailleur at twenty miles per hour.

If you ask any of these cyclists about any of these things, they'll tell you they're just doing their jobs.

"Your bike is your wife, your master, it's your best friend and all you want to do is succeed. And you don't think you are getting older and you don't think about what happens at home or with your family or who pays the bills. You don't mature because, on the road, life is going at 110 miles an hour and you don't have time to think how the world actually moves."
—**Stephen Roche**

"This is a pretty extreme occupation—it isn't the kind of job you can separate from the rest of your life. It completely affects your health, your habits."
—**Travis Brown**

"You're not allowed to own clothes without logos. My dad thinks that I have a Miyata logo sewn on the back of my Fruit-of-the-Looms."
—**Greg Herbold**

"It's your job. You have a responsibility to race your best every time for your team, and like any other job, sometimes you don't feel all there. The only problem is that you can't fake it in a race because of the physical requirements."
—**Lesley Tomlinson**

"When you choose to become a professional, you have to be young, and either naive or a megalomaniac. As for me, I was young, just seventeen, naive and, most of all, crazy about cycling."

—Marc Madiot

"I had nobody waiting in the feed zone, so I just carried everything. It looked as if I had a little backpack on. Many times I ran out of food, many times I ran out of water. Coming through a feed zone, once in a while I would try to snag a bottle from somebody but, more times than not, they would pull it back. I'd start to throw away an empty water bottle during a race and then I'd think, 'They cost five dollars each. This is going to cost me five dollars.'"

—Bobby Julich, on his independent 1993 season

"I think a dedicated novice racer can reasonably expect to put fifteen hard years into cycling. Sometime during those years you'll have your best moments and realize what your potential is. Generally it takes at least ten years to get your best results."

—Kent Bostick

"I've got stories just like everyone else—sleeping in parks, on people's floors, anywhere just to keep racing. I'd like to make a great living at this, be able to buy a home and things like that, but that's probably not going to happen. I race because I love racing my bicycle."

—**Chris Horner**

"Spanish."

 —**Stephane Heulot,** when asked what he learned
   during three years as a disgruntled domestique
   for the Miguel Indurain-led Banesto team

"A sponsor likes a top finisher, but a top finisher with a bad attitude doesn't go as far as a midpacker with an awesome attitude."

—**Jake Orness**

"There are two ways to have a good career. One is to be a champion. The other is to be a great team rider, because a good team rider always finds work. Me, I wanted to become, how do you say, indispensable."

 —**Bjarne Riis,** on winning the 1996 Tour de France

"Snow, for sure it was snowing, for sure it was cold, but I was paid to pedal."

    —Bernard Hinault, on winning the Liege-Bastogne-
        Liege classic road race

"I regret I am not racing anymore because it was a very sane life—more real than now. Normally in life we're obliged to say 'yes' when we mean 'no.' That is not so in racing. As a racer, a 'yes' is 'yes' and 'no' is 'no.'"

    —Felice Gimondi

"My mom is psyched. It's the last time she has to come and watch me race."

    —Sara Ballantyne, at her final pro race

"When I add it all up there are hundreds of reasons why I should stop and only one reason for carrying on: money. I could earn in one year what it would take six years to earn in a normal job. But that's the only reason I have to continue, and it's not enough."

    —Stephen Roche, retiring

"Cycling had been my life for twenty years. I lived it every minute of the day and there was nothing in my life that wasn't involved in my cycling. I wasn't a super champion, but I fought an epic battle trying to be one."

—Allan Peiper

"If you want to be a messenger? I would paraphrase a friend: It's a dead-end job for losers. You're gonna get hurt. You'll get hit by cars. The glamour is bullshit. It's a way to knock yourself out and use your body up. Of course, that's true. But it's also true that it's a lot of fun."

—Markus Cook

"They don't get the type of benefits most jobs offer. But most messengers exult in the fact that they make a living riding their bikes. That's their job benefit."

—Saida Benguerel

"When I was a bike messenger I rode Paris-Roubaix every day. I would hang on and pedal through the roughest streets."

—Nelson Vails

"The offices the girl rode between were electronically conterminous—in effect, a single desktop, the map of distances obliterated by the seamless and instantaneous nature of communication. Yet this very seamlessness, which had rendered physical mail an expensive novelty, might as easily be viewed as porosity, and as such created the need for the service the girl provided. Physically transporting bits of information about a grid that consisted of little else, she provided a degree of absolute security in the fluid universe of data. With your memo in the girl's bag, you knew precisely where it was; otherwise, your memo was nowhere, perhaps everywhere, in that instant of transit."

—**William Gibson,** on a bicycle messenger, in
Virtual Light

"The bike market isn't such a golden opportunity that you can just dive in and get rich. It's a tough market for anybody, especially a small company. To even stand a chance, you have to stand for something."

—**Grant Petersen**

"This job brought me a lot, except on the intellectual level, where I felt I regressed, and that was my biggest sacrifice."

—**Laurent Fignon**

"Bad pros make more than good amateurs."
  —Greg LeMond

"It doesn't take long for the realities of pro cycling to sink in—that cycling at the top level is no longer a pleasurable sport but a seedy business."
  —Paul Kimmage

"We went too far, I think. You don't enjoy cycling any more. Look at the speeds we do. The season is never-ending. You have to train so much, you have to be so skinny, if you eat a piece of cake you're overweight."
  —Max Sciandri

"Within the group, other racers never gave me gifts. Quite the contrary, the more my popularity rose, the more misery they heaped upon me."
  —Raymond Poulidor

"In the middle of the group, I felt like a stranger."
  —Rik van Looy

"I have to ask you to stop your riders using mobile phones during the race."

—Jean-Marie Leblanc, Tour de France director, in a pre-stage meeting with team managers

"Some guys only live for the bike. I give it two hundred percent, after all, it's how I eat. But that doesn't mean it's the only thing in my life."

—Stephane Heulot

"Dietrich Thurau didn't have the same urgent necessity as Bernard Hinault or Francesco Moser to win races. He preferred only to earn his living, and never lied about it."

—Philippe Brunel, in *An Intimate Portrait of the Tour de France*, on the world champion and six-day-race star who never fulfilled his potential

"I dedicate this victory to God, my mother, my family and those who pay me."

—Chepe Rodriguez

"It's our job as riders to keep this a soul sport. If we do it for love, we can. Our sponsors have their own agenda but riders should keep the sport what it was and is."

—**Missy Giove**

ADVENTURE

"The world lies right beyond the handlebars of any bicycle."

—Daniel Behrman, *The Man Who Loved Bicycles*

One of the beauties of the bike is that it is not just a toy and not just an exercise machine. It is also a vehicle. It can take you places. When you're young the bike helps you discover the world past the sidewalk, beyond the next block, and off to the horizon (if you have trusting parents). Even after you're all grown up, your bike will still be young and begging to find out what's around the next corner.

But as you age—as you become a certified adult with a job and a residence and a neighborhood of your own choosing—the bike also becomes a vehicle for exploring your own world. Your bike helps you discover the wonders of your backyard—the stuff you would miss in your rush to find what lies past the horizon.

I've ridden the lava fields of Mt. St. Helens, a freaky moonscape of white and black where the trail of packed pumice was marked with cairns of blacker rock. Stray away from these unsettling altars and your wheels would sink into a loose sea of rocks shot through with pinholes. I've been caught in floods in California, riding around mudslides and chancing my way through water that pounds your wheels like something furious at being woken from hibernation. I've ridden across France and into Belgium, eight days at a hundred miles per day, and up the Natchez Trace, a rolling Southern scenic highway blazed as a footpath by Native Americans. I've crossed most of Vermont in a single day. I've even ridden Indiana cornfields in a blizzard.

I'm thankful for every far-flung adventure—even the ones that seemed boring at the time. Even the ones that went horribly wrong. (With enough time, those become the best of all.) My bike has helped me experience intimacies of foreign worlds I would have seen distantly—if at all—from the seat of a car.

But, still, my favorite places to ride begin at my back door.

The Powder Valley road ride drops through a canopy of trees that keeps the untrafficked tarmac cool and shaded even in August. Tower Road will cripple your knees for a week. There's the Church Climb ride I love so much for the descents, and the Orchard ride with its fresh peaches. I love these rides for the ritual, because I know their names and they know mine. I love South Mountain, which isn't really much of a mountain—a few hundred acres of rideable land, perhaps 600 feet of altitude gain. But on its twisty, interlocking technical trails I've learned as much about myself as I have about how to ride a mountain bike.

Cyclists will always need new adventure, fresh trails and strange places. But we also need a home—a route we know as well as we know ourselves, a friend who waits for us and calls us to come out and play.

"I delighted in the supreme sense of freedom that comes with the first mile of a bicycle journey. No bills, no messy relationships, no job. All I needed was stuffed into four sturdy panniers."

> —**Dan Buettner,** on beginning his 12,000-mile, 277-day ride across Africa

"To travel by bicycle is a humble, nonagressive way to get close to people. It is a way of saying we are passing through with no thought of invasion or conquest, only the simple will to share a part of the road."

> —**Claude Herve**

"A bicycle ride is a flight from sadness."

> —**James E. Starrs,** *The Noiseless Tenor*

"In Bangkok, I jumped into a bicycle taxi. The driver, a 21-year-old named Tik, uses his powerful legs to take me around. I bought him lunch and asked if I could take him for a ride. On a wide stretch of road, we switched places. It was hard to get started but soon we were gliding. The steering was sluggish and the seat uncomfortable. But behind me in the tropical sun, Tik was enjoying his ride."

—**Ray Hosler**

"He always took his bicycle when he went into the country. It was part of the theory of exercise. One day one would get up at six o'clock and pedal away to Kenilorth, or Stratford-on-Avon—anywhere. And within a radius of twenty miles there were always Norman churches and Tudor mansions to be seen in the course of an afternoon's excursion. Somehow they never did get seen, but all the same it was nice to feel that the bicycle was there, and that one fine morning one really might get up at six."

—**Aldous Huxley,** *Crome Yellow*

"Your eye for geography grows sharp. Your legs attend the lost world of contours, the dales and hills that are ironed out by internal combustion."

—**Chip Brown,** "A Bike and a Prayer"

"Like a good story, every good ride has a beginning, a middle and an end. Rides always have a beginning, even when you're with textbook dawdlers, and always have an end, even when you're suffering a ceaseless case of chamois chafe. Where they go really bad is when they lack a good middle. A ride without a good middle is a like an Oreo filled with nothing but spit and dust. Smart riders know that the best way to ensure a good middle is to stop and enjoy a rest break."
—**Rob Story**

"Tour books are like cookbooks, to be used when in doubt."
—**James E. Starrs,** *The Noiseless Tenor*

"I did not ride for pleasure. I rode to get somewhere, and I don't mean from the house on San Benito Avenue in Fresno to the Public Library there. I mean I rode to get somewhere myself."
—**William Saroyan,** *The Bicycle Rider in Beverly Hills*

"The next three evenings, for it was well in to summer, I rode a dozen miles out into the country, where fresh air smelt like cowshit and the land was colored different, was wide open and windier than in streets. Marvelous. It was like a new life starting up, as if till then I'd been tied by a mile-long rope round the ankle to home."

—**Alan Sillitoe,** "The Bike"

"I am a lot more committed to encouraging the love of cycling and the self-reliance of being able to improve your own bike than I am to that vitality-robbing suggestion that you must lay out big bucks in order to 'keep up' with other riders."

—**Leonard Zinn,** *Mountain Bike Performance Handbook*

"To the bicycle tourer, one minute's realism is worth an hour's imaginings, preparatory to the event."

—**James E. Starrs,** *The Noiseless Tenor*

"Distance measured with a pair of compasses is not precisely the same as when measured by the leg."

—**Jerome K. Jerome,** *Three Men on the Bummel*

"It is by riding a bicycle that you learn the contours of a country best, since you have to sweat up the hills and coast down them. Thus you remember them as they actually are, while in a motor car only a high hill impresses you, and you have no such accurate remembrance of country you have driven through as you gain by riding a bicycle."

—**Ernest Hemingway,** *By-Line*

"The journey back was even more eerie than the journey out, the moon now behind them, their shadows before, and as they climbed the hills the mountains climbed before them as if to bar their way and when they rushed downward to the leaden bowl that was the lake, and into the closed gully of the coom, it was as if they were cycling not through space but through a maw of Time that would never move."

—**Sean O'Faolain,** *Silence of the Valley*

"We all possess a predilection for lostness, some of us more than others. But lostness, like all talents, must be nurtured, developed and practiced in order to enjoy its benefits. Many of my friends know where they have been, where they are and where they are headed. How sad."

—**Marla Streb**

"A bicycle trip may be a lonely, even a daring adventure, but the companionship of two wheels under foot establishes a silent and fortifying partnership. A bicycle journey may be longer and more arduous than travel by car, but, with time, distance evaporates in the elation of personal achievement. A bicycle tour may be faster than travel by foot, but its speed is the measured, rhythmic pace of one who, after James Stephens, has 'quit forever more the brick-built den' that hides us from all contact with our fellow men."

—**James E. Starrs,** *The Noiseless Tenor*

"The bicycle also is an amulet against various disorders. To see before one a forked or meandering road, a wedge-towered Norman church in the valley, to explore the fragrance of lanes like green tunnels, to hear the whispering hum beneath you and the rasp of scythes in a hayfield, all this might well be homeopathic against passion, for it is a passion itself."

—**Christopher Morley,** *The Romany Stain*

"It is no exaggeration to affirm that a journey by bicycle is like none other; it is a thing apart; it has a tempo and a style of its own."

—**James E. Starrs,** *The Noiseless Tenor*

"The best rides are the ones where you bite off much more than you can chew, and live through it."
—**Doug Bradbury**

"My idea of a good mountain bike ride is one in which speed, time and distance are forgotten. It's supposed to be a renewing experience—one that takes you, not one that pulls you back and reminds you."
—**Gary Wockner,** *Gold Hill and Back*

"I think that the best rides are the ones that scratch some indelible cycling imprint into your brain that you can call up on a gray March afternoon when the world seems about to end. 'You remember that time when we were riding back from . . . ?' The distance is less important sometimes than some particular occurrence but long, tiring rides seem to impart the most memories."
—**Christopher Koch**

"I want to know different environments. I want to ride to them and completely immerse myself in them. It restores me."
—**Thom Parks**

"Passing softly through the backcountry creates a fascinating tension. On one hand is the environment, generating powerful swells of energy that course through our psyches. There's something about mountains, deserts, woods, that excites us. Yet, on the other hand, the awesomeness of it all diminishes our importance in the earth's affairs."
—Hank Barlow

"The bicycle can be a philosophical tool quite as readily as it is a locomotive one. While I don't see anything wrong with the use of bikes for sport, I do get very bored with the way in which the sporting mentality has penetrated every corner of the cycling world. Many cycle tourists, seduced into seeing themselves as just another breed of athlete, wear funny clothes to prove they are serious about it, and plan their trips as just another kind of race: A to B, quickly as possible. There must be more to life than this."
—Gareth Lovett Jones

"A ten-day, thousand-mile bicycle trip, in the telling, becomes a five-day, two-thousand-mile trip."
—James E. Starrs, *The Noiseless Tenor*

"Any traveling cyclist can relate the feeling of carefree abandon and catharsis that pedaling evokes as layers upon layers of mental and emotional encrustations are shed. Each turn, each hill is another discovery illuminating a place, a sensation and a perception until then hidden from view. Nothing is so utterly alive and well as the spirit of the traveler on a bicycle."

—**James E. Starrs,** *The Noiseless Tenor*

"Movement. On a cross-country ride, it's your lifeblood."

—**Frosty Woolridge**

"As you become a creature of the road, it mostly feels mundane. It takes perspective to erase the routine and recall all the glory moments, all the wondrous feelings of uninhibited travel and of distance that become a physical part of you, like an extra network of tendons and blood vessels in your legs. It doesn't feel heroic to cross the continent; it feels poetic."

—**David M. Abramson**

"Bicycles have no walls."

—**Paul Cornish**

EQUIPMENT

"The bicycle is something to every person. Something else, that is. To me it is, for starters, movement, music, departure, arrival, design, poetry, art, health, fun. But most of all, it is this incredible machine that involves two wheels, a pipe frame, handlebars, seat, hangar (if that's the spelling of the word), pedals and chain. You get on this simple machine, you hold the handlebars, you press down on the pedals with your feet, and you go."

—William Saroyan

EQUIPMENT

When I was an editor at *Bicycling* magazine I got to work and ride with Jim Langley, who is not only the best mechanic in the world but cares about bikes more than anybody I know. I don't mean that Jim loves cycling more than anyone else, or that he knows more about bicycles than everyone. (Although both of those things are possible—he's the kind of guy who restores high-wheelers but can also rebuild a full-suspension bike dissembled down to the tiniest washer without previously seeing the thing intact.)

What I'm trying to describe is something in Jim that I haven't seen in any other cyclist in quite the same way—a kind of bikish empathy. When Jim sees a bike he doesn't see just a bike. He sees each part of the bike and he understands intuitively what each part of the bike does and how—yet at the same time it's not a disjointed vision, and not one that's solely mechanical. He knows that each bike has a personality, and an ancestry, and its own stories, if that makes any sense at all. It's not quite as freaky in reality as I make it sound here. I'm just trying to say that Jim relates to the human part of the machine, the part most of us can see only in our own, oldest and most loyal bikes. (Conversely, sometimes when he looks at riders I get the feeling he is learning something about their bikes as well.)

I think of this when I'm hours into what should have been a simple mechanical procedure, frustrated that the bike seems to be fighting me, that all the tiny pieces are conspiring to stay apart. Or when the opposite occurs and the rabbit leaps from the hat—like when I change a flat and unseat the tire from the rim with my bare hands the way Jim taught me.

It's not expertise and surgical skill with a box wrench that inspire me so much. I've learned those qualities from other great mechanics. Those wrenches are my saints, and I seek their guidance religiously, and probably more regularly than they'd wish. But Jim is something else, like the god of bike equipment, and for that this chapter is dedicated to him—and to the people like him that all of you must know, the important people who remind us that the bike itself is as beautiful a thing as the ride.

"The bicycle is a curious vehicle. Its passenger is its engine."
  —John Howard

"The sheer humanity of the machine: It uses the right muscles (those of the thighs, the most powerful in the body) in the right motion (a smooth rotary action of the feet) at the right speed (60 to 80 revolutions per minute)."
  —Stuart S. Wilson

"It's the first machine we master as children and the one we abandon when the seductions of the automobile take over."
  —Colman McCarthy

"A bicycle hides nothing and threatens nothing. It is what it does, its form is its function."
  —Stewart Parker, *Spokesong*

"A raggedy ride beats a dressed-up walk."
  —Simon Peat

"The bicycle is ergonomically tailored to the human form and psyche, yet I wonder if a hithero 'undiscovered' native tribe, when presented with a bicycle, would ever be able to determine what on earth it was for."

—**Borin Van Loon**

"The essence of bicycling is the beauty of the machine itself. The technical simplicity, the light weight, the slowly advancing trick components—that's absolutely as much of the beauty and joy of cycling as the fact that the guy on the bike happens to be a physical machine with muscles."

—**Jack Lambie**

"Of all the sports, cycling is the one that requires the most perfect match of man and machine. The more perfect the match, the more perfect the result."

—**Paul Cornish**

"A big lie is that frame material is the most important factor in determining how a bike rides. That's not true. Frame design is most important. You can get almost any material to do anything."

—**Grant Petersen**

"Winning is the best deodorant. Someone can look at your bike and say it stinks, but if you win with it, suddenly it's okay."
—**Jim Busby**

"Ask a scientist to design a better violin and you get a dirty look. While the instrument seems simple, the science behind it is not. Such is bicycle stability: The machine appears uncomplicated but the theories governing its motion are nightmarish. Some things just can't be easily defined by physics and mathematics. The interactions of the body, mind, muscles, terrain, gravity, air and bicycle are so complex that they defy exact mathematical solutions. The feel and handling of a bike borders on art. Like the violin, it's been largely designed by touch, inspiration and experimentation."
—**Chester Kyle**

"The bicycle was the last advance in technology everybody understands. Anybody who can ride one can understand how it works."
—**Stewart Parker,** *Spokesong*

"Fathered by the remnant of a dying feudal system, mothered by the still young Industrial Revolution, the bicycle—with the horny-handed, ever-present human curiosity and inventiveness as mid-wife—was born around about the tail end of the eighteenth century."
—**Seamus McGonagle,** *The Bicycle in Life, Love, War and Literature*

"I love full suspension, although the extra weight is a bummer. My hardtail weighs about three pounds less, but the advantages of rear suspension are so great that I'd like to use it all the time."
—**John Tomac**

"Rigid bikes are cool. Wraparound sunglasses and old Levi's 501s cool. Timelessly cool. Suspension may be the future. Suspension may make it easier to bomb scary trails without the aid of any skill, but rigid bikes are still the beauty and soul of riding."
—**Mike Ferrentino**

"My coaster-brake bike lays certain restrictions on you. I like that. You have to get off and walk sometimes. You have to descend slowly. It makes you see what you're doing, why you're riding."

—**Bob Seals**

"Riding among the bicycles of Beijing, I recognized dozens of China's famous brands: Golden Lion and Mountain River, Plum Flower and Chrysanthemum, Red Flag and Red Cotton, Flying Arrival and Flying Pigeon, Phoenix and Forever. Long and stately bikes, recalling decades past, they possessed the rake, sheer and grace that today I associate less with cycling than with yachting. I felt as if I were cruising on the wake of clippers."

—**Fred Streibeigh**

"Bicycles may change, but cycling is timeless."

—**Zapata Espinoza**

"The gross and net result of it is that people who spend most of their natural lives riding iron bicycles over the rocky roadsteads of this parish get their personalities mixed up with the personalities of their bicycle as a result

of the interchanging of the atoms of each of them and you would be surprised at the number of people in these parts who nearly are half people and half bicycles. . . . And you would be flabbergasted at the number of bicycles that are half-human almost half-man, half-partaking of humanity."
—**Flann O'Brien,** *The Dalkey Archive*

"The oneness of the bike takes precedence over the oneness of being."
—**William Nealy,** *Mountain Bike!*

"Are light bikes always faster than heavy bikes? Ask the question this way: Do you ride more slowly with full water bottles—which weigh more than a pound each—than empty ones? I don't know about you, but I don't see myself getting faster as I drain my bottles. But that's not to say bike weight doesn't matter. The perception exists that some bikes ride heavy and some ride light, and I think the difference has something to do with where the weight is. Bike weight, while easily quantified, is not as easily judged. Riding a bike is more than a physics problem. A twenty-pound bike that is heavy in the wrong places is not going to ride as well as a twenty-pound bike with better weight distribution."
—**Doug Roosa**

"If we can make the rider forget that the bike is there, we have done our job."
  —**Doug Martin**

"So perfect is the safety bicycle, that, if the rider has sufficient skill not to interfere with its action, it will travel straight ahead and keep its own balance."
  —*Scientific American,* 1896

"Bicycles are pretty weird. The conventional bicycle is a very potent and instantly recognizable symbol, if not icon, yet, how did the most efficient mode of human transport develop such an idiosyncratic shape?"
  —**Borin Van Loon**

"Our industry has fallen too much in love with the extreme aspect of the sport—flying down the side of the mountain at breakneck speeds in your underwear! It's not about flying down the mountain; it's the joy of being on top of the mountain."
  —**Horst Leitner**

"Bicycle designers and engineers must ride. If they do not, there's no way they can fathom the stresses the stuff is exposed to."
—Bob Gregario

"Light. Strong. Cheap. Pick two."
—Keith Bontrager

"We have to free ourselves from history but not lose the mind behind the Italian bike. The Japanese could make a bike that pedals itself and we'd still sell our share of Italian bikes."
—Romano Pisi

"It's as if a great hand swept through Europe, gathering seeds from that passionate home of the bicycle, then crossed the Atlantic and sowed those sweet kernels in North America. Not since the turn of the century have so many artisans been busy at work on the perfection of the bicycle."
—Ted Costantino

"A thin hoop of extruded aluminum is laced to a hub with a handful of steel spokes that exert a collective force of several tons. A pair of these structures can support up to 500 times their weight, sustain repeated pounding from the road or trail, endure substantial side loads during cornering, and transmit pedaling and braking torque. All this while remaining true to within a fraction of a millimeter."
   —**Doug Roosa**

"I've always considered the bike wheel to be the most ingenious single mechanical contrivance of all human engineering."
   —**Eric Hjertberg**

"The bike wheel is a bagel, waiting to be crushed."
   —**Pino Morroni**

"People say they can sense a difference between three- and four-cross wheels, but I think what they're really sensing is something acoustic, not any differences in stiffness. We haven't been able to measure it."
   —**Jon Hjertberg**

"The most primitive bike part is the chain. With gates, ramps, chain links and better shift levers we have improved the way bikes shift gears. But we still have a chain that has to run through the mud and then go from gear to gear. Everything else is so high-tech. But the chain is so primitive."

—Ned Overend

"We cannot remain mesmerized by such things of doubtful utility as a chain with pins that don't stick out. Why not invent a rustproof chain that never needs lubrication?"

—Scott Matthews

"My philosophy is really very simple: I design machines that help people get out in nature. My inventions just help make it more fun for people, no matter how strong or skilled."

—Horst Leitner

"I think that I should rather like
to be the saddle of a bike."

—John Betjeman

There may be a better land where bicycle saddles are made of rainbow, stuffed with cloud; in this world the simplest thing is to get used to something hard."

—Jerome K. Jerome, *Three Men on the Bummel*

"Tubulars are like drugs and motorcycles. People use 'em because they're attracted to the danger."

—Eric Hjertberg

"Variable gears are only for people over forty-five. Isn't it better to triumph by the strength of your muscles rather than by the artifice of a derailleur? We are getting soft. Give me a fixed gear."

—Henri Desgrange, 1903

"Sometimes jerseys are even uncool. The guys that have a bike and a helmet and that's it, they're my favorite mountain bikers."

—Dave Wiens

"I've got new shoes on today, so watch out!"

—Frederic Moncassin

Hey diddle, diddle
The bicycle riddle—
The strangest part of the deal.
Just keep your accounts
And add the amounts
The 'sundries' cost more than the wheel.
   —Anonymous 1896 poem

"The type of valve you have on your tire is determined by the type of fitting you have on your pump. For example, if your pump is equipped with a presta attachment, then your tires inevitably have schrader stems."
   —Mike Keefe, *The Ten Speed Commandments*

"There are two ways you can get exercise out of a bicycle: You can overhaul it or you can ride it. On the whole, I am not sure that a man who takes his pleasure overhauling does not have the best of the bargain."
   —Jerome K. Jerome, *Three Men on the Bummel*

★

"I rented a bike partly out of convenience, partly because I had been neglecting my old Bridgestone so much that the damn thing would probably relish the chance to go after my collarbone."
—**David Story**

"I used to work in a bike shop a long time ago in Colorado. I didn't know anything about bikes. I thought that when you had a flat tire you had to replace the whole bike."
—**Juli Furtado**

"I relax by taking my bicycle apart and putting it back together again."
—**Michelle Pfeiffer**

"Few businesses match the marvelous choreography of a smooth-running bicycle store—the musty rubber smell, the incessant phones, hissing compressors and clamorous, freewheeling bikes."
—**Jim Langley**

"The mechanic with a little mileage on the treads sees dirt as a benign presence, a good thing. He or she knows that if something breaks, a clean part will replace the broken one, and will eventually get dirty like everything else. The dirt is rarely responsible for any breakage or failure. It's all very Zen."

—Mike Ferrentino

"Cleaning a bike's like cleaning a toilet. If you do it regularly, it's fine and easy. If you wait, it's a truly disgusting experience."

—Steve Gravenites

"One measurement is worth a thousand expert opinions."

—Donald Sutherland

"Few people realize that when you move the seatpost an innocent inch or two you are changing the action of every muscle in the lower limb which is involved in the pedaling action."

—Peter R. Cavanagh

"I really love the mountain bike industry because there's just so much room for new ideas. It's similar to the aircraft industry back in the late 40s through the 50s. They came up with wild things: airplanes that took off straight up, putting the wheels on the fuselage—anything you could imagine. It's like that now with mountain bikes. All the manufacturing going on is really an art. It's a form of expression."

—Bob Barnett

"There are so many fads in this sport. One good way to figure out if something is a fad is if it costs a lot."

—George Mount

"How can we tell the fads from the genuine improvements? A splendid litmus test is the acceptance of new products by professional racers. Pros are a conservative breed. They realize that components may not win races, but component failures certainly lose races. So above all they want reliable equipment. After six or seven hours of intense effort and concentration, nobody is going to risk dropping the chain in the final sprint."

—Frank Berto

"Friction has a bad reputation in cycling, but without it you wouldn't get far. In fact, your bike would fall apart. The seat, headset and most of the bolts would loosen, the chain would skip, and without tire traction you wouldn't even be able to get started."
—**Chester Kyle**

"If there's going to be any advance in human-powered flight, it's going to be in blimps."
—**Bryan Allen**

"The longer you've been racing, the less importance you place on equipment. Someone who's a new racer finds the bicycle a real attraction—all the new equipment and all that. But it gets kind of old after awhile. You want just a good, working bike that's gonna be strong and lightweight."
—**Tom Shuler**

"It's more important who you train with than whose bike you're riding."
—**Gary Fisher**

"Pros regard their bikes as tools, not as objets d'art."
—**Fred Matheny**

"When you get to top level racing, the difference in equipment can make a difference between winning and losing, but when you're starting out it doesn't matter."
—**Greg LeMond**

"Bikes don't win races. Racers do."
—**Steve Hegg**

EVERYTHING IS BICYCLE

"Consider a man riding a bicycle. Whoever he is, we can say three things about him. We know he got on the bicycle and started to move. We know that at some point he will stop and get off. Most important of all, we know that if at any point he stops moving and does not get off the bicycle he will fall off it. That is a metaphor for the journey through life of any living thing, and I think of any society of living things."

—William Golding, *A Moving Target*

There are 1.1 billion bicycles in use around the world, give or take a few Flying Pigeons, Peugeot randonneurs, pedicab rickshaws and full-suspension titanium downhill mountain bikes. That's about one bike for every three people.

Depending on what you want to believe, the bicycle was invented sometime between 1816 and 1863 by a German forester/physicist, an English coach maker, a Scottish blacksmith hermit or two French carriage-making brothers, among others—or sketched (but never built) on the back of a notebook page by Leonardo Da Vinci sometime around 1500. The Leonardo myth is attractive, but I happen to most like the story that a poor mechanic named Pierre Lallement built the first pedal-driven bicycle in Paris in 1863, then emigrated to the United States where he patented the bicycle in 1866 and a few years later sold the patent for one thousand dollars, then lived out his life working as a machinist building for someone else the marvelous velocipede he had introduced to the world. That much is fact, for sure. You could look it up.

The point of this isn't to ring the bell for another round of historical fistfights, but to show that not only are there lots and lots and lots of bicycles surrounding us but that they've been riding alongside us for at least a century and perhaps more—long enough to be rolled right into the fabric of human life. They are not really a thing apart.

As cyclists we have a tendency to become entranced by our bike world and forget that we ride bikes in a world—kind of like not seeing a wheel because you're fascinated by the spokes. Beyond a cyclist's context of sport, fitness, travel and commuting, the bicycle means something. It meant something to Pablo Picasso, Marcel Duchamp and Keith Haring. It meant something when Paul Newman rode Katherine Ross on the handlebar in "Butch Cassidy and the Sundance Kid."

None of those images—or thousands of others—have anything to do with cycling in the sense that you and I would expect. Yet the bicycle, and the bicycling world, is greater for them. It's not only noncyclists who can see the bike this way—some riders get it, too. Our beloved machine is bigger than any of us know, and I belove it even more because it can be used to say so many things about so many things.

"It was divinely said that the kingdom of God is within you. Some make a mysticism of this declaration, but it is hard common sense; for the lesson you will learn from me is this: every kingdom over which we reign must be first formed within us on what I as a bicycle look upon as the common parade ground of individual thought."
—**Frances Willard,** *How I Learned to Ride the Bicycle*

"If the bicycle could speak, it would have much to say, presented ever so quietly and unobtrusively."
—**James E. Starrs,** *The Noiseless Tenor*

"Be at one with the universe. If you can't do that, at least be at one with your bike."
—**Lennard Zinn**

"It is easy to be a holy man on a mountain bike."
—**Mark W. Matson**

"My mother and I have a difference of opinion. She thinks I should go see a shrink; I think I should buy a new bike."
—**Alex Obbard**

"Wheel, kindly light, along life's cycle path, Wheel Thou on me! The road is rough, I have discerned Thy Wrath, But wheel me on!"
  —**Christian Hymn**

"Is it about a bicycle?"
  —**Flann O'Brien,** posing a question about the after-life in *The Third Policeman*

"Life may not be about your bike, but it sure can help you get through it."
  —**Hallman**

"Biking is my art form—my self expression."
  —**Missy Giove**

"I found a whole philosophy of life in the wooing and winning of my bicycle."
  —**Frances Willard,** *How I Learned to Ride the Bicycle*

"To possess a bicycle is to be able first to look at it, then to touch it. But touching is revealing as insufficient; what is necessary is to be able to get on the bicycle and take a ride. But this gratuitous ride is likewise insufficient; it would be necessary to use the bicycle to go on some errands. And this refers us to longer uses. . . . But these trips themselves disintegrate into a thousand appropriative behavior patterns, each one of which refers to others. Finally, as one could foresee, handing over a bank note is enough to make a bicycle belong to me, but my entire life is needed to realize this possession."

—**Jean-Paul Sartre,** *Being and Nothingness*

"Sartre much preferred riding a bicycle to walking. The monotony of walking bored him, while the intensity of effort and the rhythm of a bicycle journey varied constantly. He would amuse himself by sprinting on the hills. I would become winded and fall behind him. On level stretches, he pedaled with such indifference that on two or three occasions he landed in the ditch."

—**Simone de Beauvoir,** *La force de l'age*

"I ride my bicycle to ride my bicycle."

—**Zen proverb**

"Everything is bicycle."
—**Stephen Crane,** *Transformed Boulevard*

"The bicycle may be graceful, but it can also be frolicsome. Clowning is just another way in which the bicycle gives enjoyment."
—**James E. Starrs,** *The Noiseless Tenor*

"He walked in a nonchalant fashion, and his bicycle went with him as if it were a live thing."
—**D.H. Lawrence,** *Sons and Lovers*

"Bikes talk to each other like dogs, they wag their wheels and tinkle their bells."
—**Daniel Behrman,** *The Man Who Loved Bicycles*

"The behavior of a bicycle with a very high content of homo sapiens is very cunning and entirely remarkable. You never see them moving by themselves but you meet them in the least accountable of places unexpectedly. Did you ever see a bicycle leaning against the dresser in a warm kitchen when it is pouring outside?"
—**Flann O'Brien,** *The Dalkey Archive*

"Jason [McRoy] was a beautiful person and his friends all over the world are taking his ashes and shaking them here and there. A couple of his good friends from England even taped his ashes to the down tubes of their bikes when they rode down the World Cup course, so they sprinkled out there."
—**Missy Giove**

"All mankind is a-wheel aplenty and a person on nothing but legs feels like a strange animal."
—**Stephen Crane,** *Transformed Boulevard*

"I'm not ramming the bike stuff down his throat, but he can already say Campagnolo."
—**Joe Breeze,** on his two-year-old son

"Why should anybody steal a watch when they can steal a bicycle?"
—**Flann O'Brien,** *The Third Policeman*

"The bicycle makes summer a roomier and more intimate apartment of the year. The world nowadays is too big anyway, and most of us want to bring it closer, and personalize it."

—Henry Beetle Hough, *Singing in the Morning*

"More than any other emotion, melancholy is incompatible with bicycling."

—James E. Starrs, *The Noiseless Tenor*

"We might not learn cycling from literature, but by studying cycling's appearances in literature we can learn what people know and feel about cycling."

—John Forester

"If you only see the Bull's Head and not the saddle and handlebars from which it's made, then the sculpture loses its interest."

—Pablo Picasso, on one of his most famous works

"The bicycle, the bicycle surely, should always be the vehicle of novelists and poets."

—Christopher Morley, *The Romany Stain*

"Before I was sixteen I had many bicycles. I have no idea what became of them. I remember, though, that I rode them so hard they were always breaking down. The spokes of the wheels were always getting loose so that the wheels became crooked. The chains were always breaking. I bore down on the handlebars with so much force in sprinting, in speeding, in making quick getaways, that the handlebars were always getting loose and I was always tightening them. But the thing about my bicycles that I want to remember is the way I rode them, what I thought while I rode them, and the music that came to me."

—**William Saroyan,** *The Bicycle Rider in Beverly Hills*

"If the constellations had been named in the twentieth century, I suppose we would see bicycles."

—**Carl Sagan**

"I thought of that while riding my bike."

—**Albert Einstein,** on the theory of relativity

"A lot went through my mind. I thought about my country and how great it is, and how proud I am to represent it. I also thought about our political problems and how I hope that someday there can be world peace. It scares me to know that people are building bigger bombs—I just want to be able to ride my bike."

—**Steve Hegg,** on the winner's podium at the 1984 Olympics

"The fifth battalion of cyclists sent from the front has arrived at Tsaryoke. A joint meeting was held, and it was discovered that among the cyclists not a single man was found willing to shed the blood of his brothers, or to support a government of bourgeois land owners, said a commissioner, panting and covered with mud from his ride."

—**John Reed,** *Ten Days That Shook the World*

"One can sleep on a bike, so one should be able to die on a bike with no more trouble."

—**Alfred Jarry,** *The Supermale*

"The machine represented herewith opens up a new horizon in the vast domain of advertising, in which it seemed impossible to realize still another innovation."

—*Revue Universelle,* 1895

"To attack the pedals may be strenuous over the short run, but is an expression of trust in one's own powers, for with the bicycle everything depends on the self. Those who wish to control their own lives and move beyond existence as mere clients and consumers—those people ride a bike."
—**Wolfgang Sachs,** *For Love of the Automobile*

"Cycling provides all the big lessons in life: humility, pride, greed, discipline, grappling with the ego, and learning what your will is and when to apply it and how to apply it."
—**John Weissenrider**

"The only regret I have in my life is never learning to ride a bicycle."
—**Helen Hayes**

"What is the bicycle? Well, my bike is himself (myself)."
—**William Saroyan**

"There are a lot of Eddy Merckxes in the ghettos. The physical ability is out there."
—**Butch Martin**

"You begin pedaling—faster and faster and faster. You ease the prop pitch in, which is like shifting into a higher gear on a bicycle. Someone on the radio is shouting, 'Stay close to the center line. Stay close! Move a little more to your right. Keep your wings level.' And then the wing runner shouts, 'Okay! Looks like you're going fast enough.' You gradually ease back the stick of the airplane. And then there's that glorious moment when you take off from the runway."

—**Glenn Temml,** who pedaled the Daedalus Project into flight

"Toleration is the greatest gift of the mind; it requires the same effort of the brain that it takes to balance oneself on a bicycle."

—**Helen Keller**

"When a voodooist pictures a snake in his or her mind, or when a snake, especially a green one, appears in a dream, much sexual jealousy is felt. A bicycle seen in this same manner implies a new sexual experience. It is believed to take place with a new lover."

—**Robert W. Pelton,** *The Complete Book of Voodoo*

"Bicycles are almost as good as guitars for meeting girls."
—**Bob Weir**

Daisy, Daisy, give me your answer, do!
I'm half crazy, all for the love of you!
It won't be a stylish marriage,
I can't afford a carriage,
But you'll look sweet upon the seat
Of a bicycle built for two.
—**Harry Dacre,** "Daisy Bell"

"A young couple passed us. They rode pedal to pedal and almost arm in arm. The girl rode with her left hand on the boy's right, controlling his handlebar, steering them both. Then he moved his hand around the small of her back. They reminded me of partners in a waltz. The boy lowered his hand to the girl's saddle and leaned to her, and as they rode they whispered. In the often dehumanizing crush of urban China, two bicycles had made space for romance."
—**Fred Strebeigh**

"A woman without a man is like a fish without a bicycle."
—**Gloria Steinem**

"I like riding a bicycle built for two—by myself."
—**Harry S. Truman**

"I believe cycling should be enlightening, and its benefits should spill over into everyday life. Clearing a fallen log builds confidence, which can make it easier to ignore instruction manuals. Cleaning a steep descent expands the frontier of limitations, making it easier to gauge how long to ignore parking tickets. Learning to enjoy getting lost while mountain biking has made it easier for me to enjoy getting lost on the path of life. And that has made all the difference."
—**Marla Streb**

"A good cyclist does not need a high road."
—**Arthur Conan Doyle,** "The Adventure of the
    Priory School"

"Cycle tracks will abound in Utopia."
—**H.G. Wells,** *A Modern Utopia*

A VEHICLE
FOR REVOLUTION

"I began to feel that myself plus the bicycle equaled myself plus the world, upon whose spinning wheel we must all learn to ride, or fall into the sluiceways of oblivion and despair."

—Frances Willard, *How I Learned to Ride the Bicycle*

A Vehicle for Revolution

I'm not so sure I want bicycles to change the world. One of the reasons I love riding is because it's a little weird. We cyclists are a fringe group, buzzing along within sight but just outside the reach of the mainstream. And I like it.

I've felt a surge of prideful adrenaline when pedaling down streets so choked with other cyclists that cars can't get on—but only because of the novelty. I'd hate it if in everyday life bicycles were the things that held you up instead of allowing you to flow through traffic, if people in offices trapped you in boring discussions of chain lube the way they do with gas mileage.

I'm also not sure that bicycles can change—let alone save—the world anymore. There was a time. When the bicycle was introduced it really was a revolutionary alternative to the only other form of personal transportation besides walking: horses. You didn't have to feed a bicycle, or build or buy a stable to keep it in. You didn't need to own land to have one. Think of the impact beyond these simple economics. The bicycle made transportation possible for anyone, which meant people could travel farther for jobs, to visit places, to find love (finally allowing the gene pool to spread beyond a half-day's walk). Bikes also forced the development of road systems, because a smooth ride required something more than two carriage-wheel ruts. In 1898 membership in the League of American Wheelmen peaked at more than 141,000—still an all-time high—and in the U.S. and around the world the bicycle was poised to lead the final charge in its revolution.

And then the automobile roared to the front line. Faster, sexier, able to haul more, it reshaped the world in its image.

There was a time, but not anymore, not really. Circumstance isn't perfect and open the way it was then. Bikes won't change the world now. But they can change a life. I've seen that happen. I've seen people try commuting to work and show up the first day raving about flying past stalled traffic, or finding a quiet route by a stream you'd never see from the highway. I've seen bike commuters shed pounds, build muscle, save money and locate some hidden energy they'd thought they'd long ago lost forever. I've seen someone else notice the changes and decide to give commuting a try—or vow to ride down to the grocery the next time they need some milk. Someone else notices, and someone else, and one day they're asking their company to install showers and bike storage and. . . .

How far can these ripples travel? Far enough? Around the world there are some amazing statistics. In Holland, 29 percent of all trips are by bike. In Denmark, the figure is 18 percent. In most large cities only about 3 percent of the population travels by bike, but in Amsterdam, Copenhagen and Tokyo the figure is above twenty percent.

I'm not so sure I want bicycles to change the world. But maybe they can. Maybe they will. Maybe they are.

"Such historians as record the tides of social manners and morals, have neglected the bicycle."
—**John Galsworthy,** *The Forsyte Saga*

"The bicycle is the vehicle of a new mentality. It quietly challenges a system of values which condones dependency, wastage, inequality of mobility, and daily carnage."
—**Jim McGurn,** *On Your Bicycle*

"Each time a driver makes a trip by cycle instead of by automobile, not only the cyclist but society as a whole reaps the benefits."
—**Marcia D. Lowe,** *The Bicycle: Vehicle for a Small Planet*

"In a car you are carried; on a bike you go. You are yourself integral with the machine."

   —**Christopher Morley,** *The Romany Stain*

"Cars are all right on occasion, but they are not moments of grace, as bicycles are."

   —**Colman McCarthy**

"Is it not time we stopped riding our bikes and began to drive them? Similarly, who ever drove a car? We ride them. Words matter."

   —**Andrew Shrimpton**

"What cars are to the West, bicycles are to China: both a means of transport and a status symbol."

   —**James E. Starrs,** *The Noiseless Tenor*

"Cyclists have a right to the road too, you noisy, polluting, inconsiderate maniacs! I hope gas goes up to eight bucks a gallon!"

   —**The dad of "Calvin & Hobbes,"** responding to
      Calvin's request for traffic safety poster ideas

"Possibly the tragedy of the bicycle is that it was invented too close in time to the car. In the historical scheme, pedal power hardly got under way before the combustion engine appeared and, not only took over the roads, but changed our view of machines. We've forgotten that pedal power is a potent form of energy."
—**Richard Ballantine**

"Bicycling is a big part of the future. It has to be. There's something wrong with a society that drives a car to work out in a gym."
—**Bill Nye**

"The bicycle enables us to escape many other machines: We use it for transportation, sport, recreation, and make it a way of life."
—**Jobst Brandt,** *The Bicycle Wheel*

"I think a lot of people harbor some guilt, even if it's not on the surface, for living unsustainable lifestyles; bikes give people the opportunity to make a part of their life more sustainable."
—**Charlie Cunningham**

"Cycling is the sport of usefulness."
 —Fred DeLong

"Bicycling is human scale—a living, breathing alternative to the city's domination by motor vehicles. There is magic in blending with traffic, feeling the wind in one's face, the sheer fact of traversing the city under one's own power."
 —Charles Komanoff

"To be a real city rider, you have to learn the streets and the neighborhoods. You have to know which streets are better to ride on, which ones are safer at night. This can't be taught."
 —Keith Mills

"You haven't lived until you've put on a police uniform and hopped on a mountain bike. My daily commute became four to five minutes faster because drivers fight each other to see who gets to let me into the lane I want. Drivers would sooner cross the yellow line and hit a utility pole than breeze a cop on a bike. I've completed centuries and even won races, but this newfound respect is the sweetest cycling experience of all."
 —Allan Howard

"For the city bike to catch on we need a revolution in our society's infrastructure. Right now a city rider needs to be a road warrior, and the bike needs to be cheap and ugly so it won't get stolen. That's not a bike-friendly culture."
  —**Gary Fisher**

MY OTHER CAR IS A BICYCLE
  —**Bumper sticker**

"Government must help to eliminate cars so that bicycles can help to eliminate government."
  —**Advocacy slogan, Holland**

"The Fire Islands and the Mackinac Islands, where bicycles call the tune and automobiles pay the piper, are as rare as a broken spoke on the side of the rear wheel opposite the freewheel."
  —**James E. Starrs,** *The Noiseless Tenor*

"I ride a bicycle—not because I hate General Motors but haven't the courage to bomb an auto plant. I don't do it as a gesture of great stoicism and personal sacrifice. . . . You ride a bicycle because it feels good. The air feels good on your body; even the rain feels good. The blood starts moving around your body, and pretty soon it gets to your head, and, glory be, your head feels good. You start noticing things. You look until you really see. You hear things, and smell things you never knew were there. You start whistling nice little original tunes to suit the moment. Words start getting caught in the web of poetry in your mind. And there's a nice feeling, too, in knowing you're doing a fundamental life thing for yourself: transportation."

—Nicholas Johnson

"A cyclist can ride three-and-a-half miles on the calories found in an ear of corn. Bicycles consume less energy per passenger mile than any other form of transport, including walking. A ten-mile commute by bicycle requires 350 calories of energy, the amount in one bowl of rice. The same trip in the average American car uses 18,600 calories, or more than half a gallon of gasoline."

—Marcia D. Lowe, *The Bicycle: Vehicle for a Small Planet*

"When one compares the energy consumed in moving a certain distance as a function of body weight for a variety of animals and machines, one finds that an unaided walking man does fairly well (consuming about 0.75 calorie per gram per kilometer), but he is not as efficient as a horse, a salmon or a jet transport. With the aid of a bicycle, however, the man's energy consumption for a given distance is reduced to about a fifth (roughly 0.15 calorie per gram per kilometer). Therefore, apart from increasing his unaided speed by a factor of three or four, the cyclist improves his efficiency rating to number one among moving creatures and machines."
   —Stuart S. Wilson

THE BICYCLE WINS IF IT DOES NOT LOSE, THE AUTOMOBILE LOSES IF IT DOES NOT WIN
   —New York City graffiti

"The bicycle is a vehicle for revolution."
   —Daniel Behrman, *The Man Who Loved Bicycles*

"Few articles ever used by man have created so great a revolution in social conditions as the bicycle."
   —U. S. Census Report, 1900

"Socialism can only come riding a bicycle."
   —Jose Antonio Viera-Gallo

"Starting a bicycle industry is a relatively low-risk venture for developing countries that have little industrial base. A small assembly plant and repair shop can run on about $200 worth of tools, and a hundred bicycles can be manufactured for the energy and materials it takes to build one medium-sized car."
   —Centro Salvadoreno de Tecnologia Apropiada,
      San Salvador, 1986

"The bicycle has been an instrument of war in the hands of any political and military groups needing its capabilities. Vietcong or American, Nazi oppressor or French Resistance, the bicycle doesn't care; it stands ready to carry any and all to victory."
   —James Berryhill

"For want of a bicycle the independence of a nation may be forfeited."
　—W. C. Whitney

"There is a move afoot to destroy Congress as we know it. In the future, the kind of people who run for congress will be coming up here in sleeping bags and sleeping in their offices and riding bicycles to work."
　—Jack Brooks

"The bicycle is the common man among vehicles."
　—James E. Starrs, *The Noiseless Tenor*

"Act Bicycle! Speak Bicycle! Write Bicycle! Advise Bicycle! Impact Bicycle! Meet Bicycle! Recruit Bicycle! Persist Bicycle! Subscribe Bicycle! Communicate Bicycle!"
　—Roger Hertz

"Society is singularly in debt to the bicycle, since bicycle mechanics developed the airplane as well as the automobile."
　—James E. Starrs, *The Noiseless Tenor*

"Let a man find himself, in distinction from others, on top of two wheels with a chain—at least in a poor country like Russia—and his vanity begins to swell out like his tires."
—**Leon Trotsky**

"Yosemite National Park. At present a dusty milling confusion of motor vehicles and ponderous camping machinery, it could be returned to relative beauty and order by the simple expedient of requiring all visitors, at the park entrance, to lock up the automobiles and continue their tour on the seats of good workable bicycles supplied free of charge by the United States Government. Let our people travel light and free on their bicycles."
—**Edward Abbey,** *Desert Solitaire*

★

"Few articles ever used by man (or woman) have ever created so great a revolution in social conditions."
—**Fred C. Kelly**

WOMEN IN CYCLING

"Under the bicycle's influence, wholly or in part, have wilted chaperones, long and narrow skirts, tight corsets, hair that would come down, black stockings, thick ankles, large hats, prudery and fear of the dark; under its influence, wholly or in part, have bloomed weekends, strong nerves, strong legs, strong language, knickers, knowledge of make and shape, knowledge of woods and pastures, equality of sex, good digestion and professional occupation—in four words, the emancipation of women."

—**John Galsworthy,** *Forsyte Saga*

The story of women and cycling is more than a story of sport. From the beginning—around the 1890s when the dangerous highwheeler was replaced with the smaller, steadier and simpler "safety" bicycle that resembles what we ride today—bikes meant freedom for women. Equality. Choice.

With a bike, a woman could travel solo. She could travel without waiting for a man to hitch horse to carriage. This might sound patronizing from our twentieth-century hindsight, but it's fact. Bicycles also forced dress reform. On a horse a woman could ride sidesaddle in a long skirt. But a bike required a divided skirt or bloomers, and the action of pedaling started the slow movement to shed waist-pinching corsets.

These changes shocked society. Doctors (men) and social experts (also men) predicted that exposure to speed and freedom would unhinge their sheltered women—making them promiscuous, uncontrollable, inflaming their sexual urges from the constant pressure of the saddle against the genitals. I'm not making this up. You can find it in old medical journals.

Today, the bicycle is still a gender equalizer, though its work is subtler. I see it every time my short, lean wife, Beth—with a great weight-to-leg-strength ratio—begins a glide uphill that appears relaxed but is actually a kind of smooth torture. Guys who haven't ridden with us before will sprint until they puke trying to hang with her. She's so small. And she's a woman . . .

It's also cool that some of mountain bike racing's most popular stars are women. This never happened on the road or track (which is particularly frustrating if you're an American cycling fan because some of the world's most dominant road and track riders are U.S. women). But racers such as Juli Furtado and Missy Giove get as many cheers—and as much respect—as any of the legendary men. Finally.

Of course there are still problems. Women's prize money in races is dismal. And most bikes aren't built for women—the frame proportions are based on men's longer torsos, so the top tubes are too stretchy for some women to ride with comfort and control. Then there are the testosterone-based ad campaigns whose comparisons of bikes to penises, testicles, and getting lucky discourage some women from exploring the sport.

In the 1890s and early 1900s, women smashed through roadblocks by organizing, protesting and rebutting ridiculous assertions with plain facts. But part of the solution was just riding. I think that's a good solution, today, too. Every time a woman makes a guy taste his own lungs on a ride, a little more of the problem is solved.

"The girl in bloomers is, of course, upon her native heath when she steers her steel steed into the boulevard."
—**Stephen Crane,** *Transformed Boulevard*

"Let me tell you what I think of bicycling. I think it has done more to emancipate women than anything else in the world. It gives women a feeling of freedom and self-reliance. I stand and rejoice every time I see a woman ride by on a wheel . . . the picture of free, untrammeled womanhood."
—**Susan B. Anthony**

"Using our own power riding bicycles is symbolic not only of a woman's need to have power over her body, but also of her ability to possess that power."
—**Andrea Rose Askowitz**

"What enjoyment to a cramped and warped woman's life is the whirl of the wheel, bringing back as it does God's gift of health, and the memory of childhood's delight in out of door activity. With a sense also of rest to the brain, and by raising the thoughts in gratitude above the household cares and drudgery, it gives a woman for one brief while the chance to rejoice in the feeling of liberty and delight in her own strength."

—*Wheelwoman,* 1896

The wheels go round without a sound—
The maidens hold high revel;
In sinful mood, insanely gay,
True spinsters spin adown the way
From duty to the devil!

—From a poem by John William Yope

"The bicycle was the first machine to redefine successfully the notion of what is feminine. The bicycle came to symbolize something very precious to women—their independence."

—Sally Fox

"In all probability the most lasting social consequence of the bicycle craze was the effect it had on American women. . . . The drive to wear 'rational dress' in the 1890's . . . was a much greater blow in behalf of the emancipation of women than taking off a brassiere."

—**Robert Smith**, *A Social History of the Bicycle*

"I've seen women who've gotten into mountain biking who really come alive after just a few months. They're radiant, they've lost weight, their shoulders are back, and they're no longer taking any crap from their husbands."

—**Carol Waters**

"There's something about getting grimy and sweaty with the gals. You feel like you're breaking the rules. You're not made of sugar and spice and everything nice. You're not someone's girlfriend and you're not someone's mother. For that moment, at least, all you have to be is a cyclist."

—**Kimberly Grob**

"Any body type can be fit to a bicycle and any person, regardless of age or sex, can excel on one. In fact, a smart woman can be competitive against a stronger man simply by using common sense and intuition."

—**Connie Carpenter Phinney**

"It's something of a myth that women are exclusively attracted to the scenic aspects of mountain biking—though I think guys need to learn how to enjoy those things a lot more. I've seen women happiest when they accomplish things like lifting their front wheels, bunny-hopping, doing a power slide."
—**Cindy Whitehead**

"Racing is not for everyone, but there are more opportunities out there for women my age to be successful because there are fewer of us. I'd tell any woman who has kids and a job that mountain bike racing is something you can do for yourself."
—**Kathy Sessler**

"Don't be afraid of ignoring people's expectations of you. Don't be afraid of going fast and getting hurt. You can always wear black stockings to cover up the scars! You just have to forget what your parents taught you—stuff like being careful, looking good and catching the best man available."
—**Marla Streb**

"With all the mud and dirt, mountain biking helps break down the stereotypes of what women should look like."
   —**Carol Waters**

"Women who love mud too much have what it takes to transform mountain biking from a boy's club to a human's club."
   —**Jacquie Phelan**

"If I had a dollar for every time one of my male riding friends whined about how few women ride seriously, I could buy some new titanium widget for my bike every week—but I wouldn't anyway, because women don't care about titanium widgets."
   —**Linda DuPriest**

"I went on a training ride with the men and I changed their attitude about women's cycling. Now they realize there are women who can race with men and even beat them, make them hurt."
   —**Marion Clignet**

"Women are attracted to cycling because they can compete with men. What women lack in muscle mass can be compensated for by savvy, willpower, and endurance. The bike is a great equalizer because the strongest are not always the best."

—Connie Carpenter Phinney

"Women's cycling is the only place where the U.S. consistently wins medals. In every other sport, the part that wins medals gets the money. In cycling, it's backwards. The part that wins medals gets—I won't say the word—but they don't get the money. It's ridiculous."

—George Mount

"City riding is a continual lesson in feminine principles, in particular the art of being vulnerable. A confrontational, macho aesthetic spells calamity. You must learn to yield, to dodge, to seek harmony. You are obliged to mind the web of interrelations, that complicated mesh of interests, conflicts, intentions."

—Chip Brown, "A Bike and a Prayer"

"Fancy a lady riding a thing like that. With a leg on each side, disturbing the traffic."
—**John Galsworthy,** *The Forsyte Saga*

"Women cyclists cannot protect their chastity."
  —**District Governor of Ramsar, Iran,**
    banning female riders

"Women seem to enjoy a distinct biological advantage when it comes to unicycling, as they are free from any supererogatory excrescencies."
  —**Jack Halpern**

"At least you can quit a bike race."
  —**Connie Carpenter Phinney,** comparing childbirth
    to competitive cycling

"I don't think I'll be riding my bike home, that's for sure."
  —**Mary Jane Reoch,** after riding to the hospital to
    give birth to a six-pound, twelve-ounce baby girl

HATE

"I think the most ridiculous sight in the world is a man on a bicycle, working away with his feet as hard as he possibly can, and believing that his horse is carrying him instead of, as anyone can see, he carrying the horse."
—**George Bernard Shaw,** *An Unsocial Socialist*

People who hate bicycles and bicyclists give me great joy.

Before I explain that, let me say that I am not talking about murderous drivers who try to run us off roads, who do hit (and kill) some of us, or throw things at us as they speed by. Such aggression has less to do with the fact that we're on bikes than that we're easy targets for sociopaths missing large parts of the human puzzle. I'm also not talking about misinformed hikers and equestrians who believe that mountain bikes have no business on trails. They're just selfish. The hatred I take delight in comes from people who despise cycling itself, people who roil and bubble with contempt for bikes and their riders—and who can say so with style.

Just before I left my job at a writer's magazine to become an editor at *Bicycling* magazine, I wrote to some of my favorite contributors to let them know where I was going and to say that I hoped we could work together on something bike-related. A guy named William Browning Spencer, who'd written a fantastic first novel called *Maybe I'll Call Anna,* wrote back to me saying he was sorry but he couldn't do anything more for me because, "I believe that bicycles are wobbly, unsound vehicles, always on the verge of becoming ensnared under buses or trucks, and often operated by humorless males wearing gaudy headgear and the sort of shiny black pants that symbolize the decline in American values and an unfortunate reverence for foreign—perhaps French—attitudes."

That's funny. We are freaks. If we're not shiny-pants asphalt freaks then we're muddy, bloody freaks who ride bikes where they're not supposed to be able to go. (If you can't see this, you need to look in a mirror after your next ride.) It's okay, you know. We chose to be this way. Only those who do not decide their destiny can't laugh at it.

But I get more than amusement from such exchanges. Ordinary things merely annoy people. Inspired hatred is one more bit of evidence that bicycles are something great, something beyond the mundane—something worthy of grand animosity. And, therefore, grand passion. As if we needed any more proof.

"If all feeling for grace and beauty were not extinguished in the mass of mankind at the actual moment, such a method of locomotion as cycling could never have found acceptance; no man or woman with the slightest aesthetic sense could assume the ludicrous position necessary for it."

—**Marie Louise de la Ramee,** *The Ugliness of Modern Life*

"Bikes are not a transportation system, never have been and never will be. They're toys."
  —Jay Craycroft

"The notion of transforming this recreation into a mode of mass transit is PC looniness of legendary proportions."
  —Brock Yates

"The ungainly geometry and primitive mechanicals of the bicycle are an offense to the eye. The grimy and perspiring riders of the bicycle are an offense to the nose. And the very existence of the bicycle is an offense to reason and wisdom."
  —P. J. O'Rourke

"Bikish chaos gratifies that instinct which is common to all stupid people, the instinct to potter with machinery."
  —Max Beerbohm, *More*

"Bicycles are a means to an end, whether that end be commuting, joy-riding or just self-punishment. I believe they are tools, instruments for enhancing our adrenaline response and general well-being. I would be the first to admit that they serve their purpose sublimely. But unfortunately, like so many other products of our techno-narcissistic society, bikes have become an end in themselves."

—Philip Johnson

"Few bicycles do realize the poster. On only one poster that I can recollect have I seen the rider represented as doing any work. But then this man was being pursued by a bull. In ordinary cases the object of the artist is to convince the hesitating neophyte that the sport of bicycling consists in sitting on a luxurious saddle and being moved rapidly in the direction you wish to go by unseen heavenly powers."

—Jerome K. Jerome, *Three Men on the Bummel*

"Tolstoy has learned to ride a bicycle. Is this not inconsistent with his Christian ideals?"

—Anton Chekov

Principal Arguments That May be Marshaled Against Bicycles
1. Bicycles are childish.
2. Bicycles are indignified.
3. Bicycles are unsafe.
4. Bicycles are un-American.
5. I don't like the kind of people who ride bicycles.
6. Bicycles are unfair.
7. Bicycles are good exercise.
   —P. J. O'Rourke

"When a driver's accelerator foot gets itchy, no one suffers more than a cyclist. Bikes and pedestrians are equally defenseless against two and half tons of pot metal, but pedestrians have an enormous advantage because they look helpless when caught in the crosshairs, and send visions of jail and bankruptcy dancing in drivers' minds. But a bike moves fast enough that, to a driver, it doesn't seem defenseless. Throw in the fact that bikes are trying to squeeze through the same choked, badly designed system of roads as cars, and drivers don't see defenseless, they see competition."

—Christopher Koch

"I want to kill a bicyclist. I want to hit one of them with my car, knock him off the road, send him spilling over the curb, tumbling out of control. I want to see the bike go flying and then—this is my fantasy—I stop the car, get out and so do all the other drivers. They cheer me. They yell 'hooray!' and then they pick me up and carry me around on their shoulders."

—**Richard Cohen**, in *The Washington Post Magazine*

"The bicycle created a new demand which was beyond the capacity of the railroad to supply. Then it came about that the bicycle could not satisfy the demand it had created. A mechanically propelled vehicle was wanted instead of a foot-propelled one, and we know that the automobile was the answer."

—**Hiram Maxim**, *Horseless Days*

"Cyclists are open-minded. Cyclists are egalitarian. Cyclists share a fellowship of the wheel that can overcome all political, social, racial and economic barriers. Except for recumbents."

—**Ted Costantino**

"In California, people seemed envious of seeing cyclists out—maybe they got beaten by their wives before they left their homes—and they sort of took it out on anybody they saw out there . . . forcing us off the road, honking at us. Even the police would be telling us to get single file, abusing us for holding up traffic."

—**Phil Anderson**

"I don't understand this sport. Why is the 200-meter sprint 1,000 meters long? What's the other 800 meters for? And why can't someone in the Tour de France make up five seconds in a stage that's ninety-seven miles long?"

—**John Scherwa**

"Mohammed was a walking Messenger. When the Moslems first saw Christian missionaries mounted upon bicycles, they stoned the gentle souls, for the contraption seemed to have come from the devil."

—**William Saroyan,** from his introduction to
The Noiseless Tenor

GENERAL CLASSIFICATION

Edward Abbey: literary writer; author of *The Monkey Wrench Gang, Hayduke Lives!* and *Desert Solitaire,* among other works. 319

Diane Ackerman: literary writer, poet, author of *A Natural History of the Senses,* among other works 20

Djamolidin Abdujaparov: pro road racer from Uzbekistan, nicknamed the "Tashkent Terror" for his fearsome sprint and even-more-fearsome pile-ups; 3-time Tour de France Points Leader (1991, 1993-94). 168

David M. Abramson: cyclist. 270

Sam Abt: cycling writer, editor of *International Herald Tribune.* 156

Henry Adams: historian; Pulitzer Prize-winning author of such works as *The Education of Henry Adams,* and *History of the United States.* 175

Paul Adkins: mountain bike instructor, tour leader and adventurer. 184

Bob Allen: cycling photographer and writer. 238

Bryan Allen: designer of the Dwarf bike blimp. 289

Norm Alvis: U.S. pro road racer; 5-time national champion; 1995 U.S. Pro road champion; 1988 U.S. Olympic team rider. 105, 134, 161

Phil Anderson: Australian pro road racer from 1980-93; winner of Kellogg's Tour of Britain (1991, 1993), and Nissan Classic/Ireland (1992). 94, 338

Frankie Andreau: U.S. pro road racer 245

Jacques Anquetil: pro French road racer; 5-time Tour de France winner (1957, 1961-64), 2-time Giro winner (1960, 1964), 9-time Grand Prix des Nations winner (1953-58, 1961, 1965-66), 5-time Paris-Nice winner (1957, 1961, 1963, 1965-66), Ghent-Wevelgem (1964), Liege-Bastogne-Liege (1966); hour record holder (46.159 km, 1956); noted climber and time-trialist. 109, 111, 112, 144, 152, 209, 215, 218, 233, 234, 236, 243

Susan B. Anthony: feminist, suffragist, equal-rights activist. 324

Franco Antonini: medical doctor. 121

Lance Armstrong: U.S. pro road racer; 2-time Tour DuPont winner (1995-96), 1993 U.S. national champion, world champion (1993), 2-time Tour de France stage winner (1993, 1995); first American to win a World Cup event (Clasica San Sebastian, 1995); first American to win a Spring Classic (Fleche Wallonne, 1996). 9, 116, 117, 239

Andrea Rose Askowitz: cyclist and women's rights advocate. 324

Greg Bagni: Schwinn product manager and promoter. 43, 175

Arnie Baker: Expert in cycling science and physiology 160

Richard Ballantine: cycling writer; author of *Bicycle* and *Richards' Ultimate Bicycle Book.* 20, 23, 312

Sara Ballantyne: U.S. pro cross-country mountain bike racer; World Cup cross-country champion (1991); national cross-country champion (1989); national downhill champion (1988). 253

Nancy Neiman Baranet: first U.S. rider to compete in a stage race in Europe (1956); 4-time national champion. 245

Hank Barlow: cycling writer. 37, 40, 190, 269

Bob Barnett: mountain bike designer. 288

Craig Barrette: BMX writer. 96

Gino Bartali: Italian pro road racer whose intense rivalry with Fausto Coppi sharply split cycling fans; 2-time Tour de France winner (1938, 1948); 3-time Giro d'Italia winner (1936-37, 1946); national champion (1935, 1937, 1940, 1952); Milan-San Remo (1939-40, 1947, 1950) 60, 215, 218, 230, 231, 240

Rick Bass: literary writer; author of numerous books, and the short story "The Watch," from which quotes are taken. 57, 85, 115

Claire Bateman: poet; author of "The Bicycle Slow Race." 85

Steve Bauer: Canadian pro road racer; 1984 Olympic silver medalist (road race), winner of Championship of Zurich (1989); like Raymond Poulidor, Bauer has a reputation for being the "eternal second," as best evidenced by his 1990 2nd-place in Paris-Roubaix, which he lost by 1 cm to Walter Planckaert. 207

Simone de Beauvoir: writer and political activist; author of *The Second Sex,* essays on existential philosophy, memoirs and the book *La force de l'age.* 296

Samuel Beckett: dramatist and novelist; works include *Waiting for Godot, Acts Without Words* and *Molloy.* 22

Max Beerbohm: critic and caricaturist; author of *The Happy Hypocrite, The Poet's Corner* and other works. 334

Daniel Behrman: literary writer; author of *The Man Who Loved Bicycles.* 51, 126, 259, 297, 316.

Saida Benguerel: San Francisco bike messenger. 254

Lord Charles Beresford: British naval officer; author of *The Betrayal.* 25

John Betjeman: poet, England's poet laureate. 283

Jean-Francois Bernard: French pro road racer; Tour de France stage winner and yellow jersey wearer (1987); Giro d'Italia stage winner (1988). 184

James Berryhill: cyclist and Vietnam veteran. 317

Frank Berto: cycling writer, technical expert. 288

James Bethea: U.S. pro cross-country mountain bike racer; former bike messenger. 38

Rudy de Bie: Beglian road, cyclocross and mountain bike pro racer. 32

Antoine Blondin: cycling writer. 113, 229, 241

Tim Blumenthal: cycling writer, executive director of the International Mountain Bicycling Association, an advocacy group that works to maintain and open trails for riding. 10, 39

Chris Boardman: English pro road and track racer; hour record holder (56.375 kilometers); Olympic pursuit champion (1992); Olympic time trial bronze medal (1996); world individual time trial and pursuit champion (1994); won prologue of Tour de France and wore yellow jersey 3 days (1994). 222

Davide Boifave: professional road racing coach and team director. 145

Keith Bontrager: bike designer and builder, founder of Bontrager Bicycles 281

Eddie B: nickname for Eddie Borysewicz, Polish cycling coach and team director who gained prominence as the U.S. national tteam coach. 55, 94, 107, 110, 168

Kent Bostick: U.S. road racer; nicknamed "Bostisaurus" after making 1996 Olympic team (4000m pursuit) at age forty-two. 121, 251

Ottavio Bottecchia: Italian pro road racer; 2-time Tour de France winner (1924-25); died mysteriously (many believe he was beaten to death) in 1927 from a fall while training alone. 60, 147, 243

Andre Boucher: trainer of Jacques Anquetil. 234

Doug Bradbury: mountain bike innovator; designer of Manitou suspension fork. 268

John Brady: U.S. pro road racer. 103

Jobst Brandt: famous wheelbuilder, coach, ride leader, author of *The Bicycle Wheel.* 138, 312

Jim Busby: bicycle designer. 276

Joe Breeze: former road and mountain-bike racer, pioneer of mountain biking, and builder of the first frame specifically designed for mountain biking; member of Mountain Bike Hall of Fame. 34, 35, 298

Harry Van den Bremt: cycling writer. 132, 233

Jack Brennan: U.S. track racer, bike shop owner and cycling historian. 242

Erik Breukink: pro road racer from the Netherlands; Olympic silver medalist (1992). 154

Jack Brooks: democratic politician from Texas. 318

Chip Brown: writer and amateur cyclist; author of the essay "A Bike and a Prayer." 24, 49, 263, 329

Travis Brown: U.S. pro cross-country mountain bike racer. 167, 202, 250

Philippe Brunel: cycling writer; author of *An Intimate Portrait of the Tour de France.* 203, 209, 218, 220, 228, 232, 233, 234, 240, 257

Johan Bruyneel: Belgium road racing pro; Tour de France stage winner (1995); wore the maillot jaune for one day in 1995. 168

Dan Buettner: professional cycling adventurer who among other treks has ridden across Africa and the former USSR and explored Mayan ruins by bicycle in MayaQuest. 262

Gianni Bugno: Italian pro road racer; world pro road champion (1991-92), Giro d'Italia (1990), Tour of Flanders (1994), 2-time winner of Tour de France stage to l'Alpe d'Huez (1990-1991). 236

Abigail van Buren: advice columnist ("Dear Abby"). 96

Edmund Burke: cycling scientist; national team consultant; author of *The High-Tech Cyclist.* 234

Jim Burlant: 22

Mike Burrows: bicycle designer. 176

Jo Burts: cartoonist. 164

Dino Buzzati: cycling writer. 231

Calvin & Hobbes: 311

Chris Carmichael: former U.S. road racer; U.S. national team coach and director. 62, 101, 160, 189, 201, 219

Connie Carpenter Phinney: U.S. road racer; junior world championship silver medalist (1977); first American Olympic gold medalist (1984); spouse of Davis Phinney. 326, 329, 330

Jon Carroll: newspaper columnist. 39, 41

Steve Casimiro: cycling writer. 36, 61, 64

Peter R. Cavanagh: biomechanics expert and professor. 287

Pierre Chany: cycling writer. 217

Anton Chekhov: Russian short story writer and novelist. 335

Claudio Chiappucci: Italian pro road racer called "Il Diablo" for his devilish, stylish attacks on the peloton; Clasica San Sebastian winner (1993), stage winner of the Tour de France (1993); third in Giro with one stage win (1993). 145, 184, 203, 228, 240

Sukeun Chun: New York City bike messenger. 83

Mario Cipollini: Italian pro road racer; extraordinary sprinter-self-proclaimed "world's fastest cyclist." 86, 87, 147, 205, 206

Marion Clignet: French road racer; French road champion (1991, 1993); world pursuit and World Cup pursuit champion (1994); French pursuit champion (1991); Olympic pursuit silver (1996). 328

John Cobb: U.S. cycling coach. 101

Richard Cohen: journalist. 337

Francesco Conconi: Italian sport-medicine specialist and cycling doctor. 102

Markus Cook: San Francisco bike messenger. 254

Steve Cook: U.S. mountain bike racer. 31

Fausto Coppi: Italian pro road racer known as "Il Campionissimo" and considered Italy's greatest rider; 4-time Giro d'Italia winner (1947, 1949, 1952-53), 2-time Tour de France winner (1949, 1952); hour record holder (45.87 km, 1942-56), Milan-San Remo (1946, 1948-49), Paris-Roubaix (1950), Fleche-Wallonne (1950), world champion (1953), Tour of Lombardy (1946-48, 1954), 4-time Italian national champion (1942, 1947, 1949, 1955); 118 career victories; Gino Bartali's greatest rival. 101, 218, 231, 232, 233, 246

Paul Cornish: U.S. road rider; first U.S. cross-country record holder (13 days, 5 hours, 20 minutes). 270, 275

Ted Costantino: cycling writer. 53, 281, 337

Edward Coyle: cycling scientist. 239

Stephen Crane: literary writer; author of *The Red Badge of Courage* and other works, including the essay, "Transformed Boulevard." 297, 298, 324

Jay Craycroft: Texas politician. 334

Don Cuerdon: cycling writer; used pen name of "Captain Dondo." 33, 42, 108, 164

Dave Cullinan: U.S. pro downhill mountain bike racer; U.S. national, Super Cup and downhill world champion (1992); first at Vail and Big Bear downhills (1993). 30, 165, 201

Charlie Cunningham: founder of Wilderness Trail Bikes; Marin County framebuilder; spouse of Jacquie Phelan. 31, 33, 185, 312

Richard Cunningham: bike designer, cycling journalist 169

Harry Dacre: composer and lyricist of "Daisy Bell," also known as "Bicycle Built for Two" (created in 1892). 304

Tom Davies: cyclist and author of Merlyn the Magician and the Pacific Coast Highway. 122

Pedro Delgado: Spanish pro road racer; 1988 Tour de France winner. 214, 215

Fred DeLong: cycling writer. 313

Susan DeMattei: U.S. pro mountain bike racer; won bronze medal at first mountain bike Olympic race (1996); spouse of Dave Wiens. 30, 188

John Derven: cyclist. 193

Henri Desgrange: originator of the Tour de France; first official hour record holder (35.325 km, 1893). 61, 284

Cindy Devine: U.S. pro mountain bike downhill racer. 187

Thomas Dickson: cycling physician, 123

Henrik Djernis: Pro cross-country mountain bike racer from Denmark; 3-time mountain bike world champion (1993-95). 103

Arthur Conan Doyle: literary author; creator of Sherlock Holmes. 21, 305

Geoff Drake: cycling writer. 53

Alison Dunlap: U.S. road and mountain bike racer; national team member; winner of Tour de France Feminin stage (1996). 87

Linda DuPriest: cycling writer and bike advocate. 328

Jacky Durand: French pro road racer known for long escapes; won 1992 Tour of Flanders. 66, 193

Jose Miguel Echavarri: Spanish coach and team director of Banesto cycling squad. 235, 236

Tom Ehrhard: U.S. cycling coach. 105

Albert Einstein: Genius. 300

Harold Elvin: writer. 84

Mike Engleman: U.S. pro road racer; noted climber; won more pro races than anyone in 1991. 62, 98

Zapata Espinoza: cycling writer; inducted into Mountain Bike Hall of Fame. 43, 136, 224, 237, 278

Francois Faber: pro road racer from Luxembourg; winner of Bordeaux-Paris (1913) and Tour de France (1909). 144

David Farmer: pro road racer. 155

David R. Farmer: U.S. mountain bike coach. 102

Michele Ferrari: pro cycling coach known for helping Francesco Moser set the hour record in 1984. 93, 104

Mike Ferrentino: cycling writer. 140, 277, 287

Laurent Fignon: French pro road racer; 2-time Tour de France winner 1983-84, Giro d'Italia (1989); 76 career victories; lost the 1989 Tour de France by 8 seconds, the slimmest margin ever, on final stage to Greg LeMond. 149, 189, 255

Sue Fish: U. S. mountain bike downhill racer. 132

Gary Fisher: mountain bike pioneer; bicycle designer. 34, 35, 166, 289, 314

John Forester: cycling advocate, safety expert, and author of landmark manual, Effective Cycling. 299

Maria Fossati: cycling writer. 242-3

Dave Fornes: U.S. road racer. 184

Alain Fournier: literary writer; author of *The Wanderer*. 45

Sally Fox: researcher of "The Sporting Woman," an art exhibit that included cyclists. 325

Nicolas Frantz: pro road racer from Luxembourg; 2-time winner of Tour de France (1927-28). 60

Thomas Frischknecht: Swiss pro cross-country mountain bike racer; cross-country World Cup champion (1992-93, 1995); silver at 1996 Olympic cross-country. 237, 239

Juli Furtado: U.S. pro cross-country mountain bike racer; U.S. national champion (1991-95); world champion and U.S. national road champion (1990); World Cup champion (1993-95); world and Super Cup downhill champion (1992); her 1993 streak of 17 victories (including all 6 national championship series races and 9 World Cup races) makes her mountain biking's Joe DiMaggio; her 30+ national and World Cup victories make her the Eddy Merckx of mountain biking. 63, 72, 93, 135, 153, 186, 200, 239, 286, 323

Francois Gachet: French pro downhill mountain bike racer; French national, world and World Cup champion (1994). 70, 76, 154

Jose Antonio Viera-Gallo: Chilean politician. 317

John Galsworthy: literary writer; author of *The Forsyte Saga*. 310, 321, 330

Raphael Geminiani: pro road racer; team director. 243

William Gibson: literary writer; author of Virtual Light. 84, 255

Felice Gimondi: Italian pro road racer; Paris-Brussels (1966, 1976), Paris-Roubaix (1966), Milan-San Remo (1974), Tour de France (1965), Giro d'Italia (1967, 1969, 1976), Vuelta a Espana (1968), world champion (1973) , Tour of Lombardy (1966, 1973), Grand Prix des Nations (1967-68); His later career was overshadowed by the beginning of Eddy Merckx's. 100, 253

Missy Giove: U.S. pro downhill mountain bike racer; world champion (1994); World Cup winner (1996). 30, 69, 71, 72, 74, 76, 109, 147, 163, 188, 201, 258, 295, 298, 323

Allison Glock: cycling writer. 39, 109, 161

Jacques Goddet: former director of the Tour de France. 60, 215, 230

William Golding: literary writer; Nobel Prize winner (1983); author of *Lord of the Flies, The Paper Men* and *A Moving Target*. 291

Ivan Gotti: Italian pro road racer. 194

Alf Goullet: Australian professional track racer (1908-25) who made his name racing in the 6-days at Madison Square Garden in the early 1900s. 225

Steve Gravenites: pro mountain bike mechanic. 76, 77, 287

Bob Gregario: pro mountain bike mechanic; John Tomac's personal wrench. 208

Claudio Gregario: cycling writer. 240

Alexi Grewal: U.S. pro road racer; Olympic road race gold medal (1984). 130, 207, 219

Rishi Grewal: U.S. pro cross-country mountain bike racer. 238

Rich Griffith: cyclist. 119

Craig Griffin: track coach from New Zealand. 96

Kimberly Grob: cycling writer. 326

Lon Haldeman: U.S. ultramarathon road racer; Race Across America winner (1982-83); spouse of Susan Notorangelo-Haldeman. 97, 118, 222, 223

Susan Notorangelo-Haldeman: U.S. ultramarathon road racer; Race Across America winner (1985, 1989); spouse of Lon Haldeman. 97

Louis J. Halle, Jr.: political scientist; author of *Spring in Washington.* 73, 82

Hallman: freaky BMX rider. 295

Jack Halpern: cycling writer; author of Anyone Can Ride a Unicycle. 330

Andy Hampsten: U.S. pro road racer; 1988 Giro d'Italia, 1987 Tour of Switzerland, only American rider to win at l'Alpe d'Huez (1992); twice 4th in the Tour de France (1986, 1992); Tour de France Best Young Rider (1986). 62, 66, 136, 189

Curt Harnett: Canadian track racer; Olympic kilometer silver medal (1984). 150

Helen Hayes: actress. 302

Steve Hegg: U.S. road and track racer; 1984 Olympic gold medalist (4000m pursuit), 1996 Olympic team member (road race, ITT); 1994 national pro road champion, 1995 national criterium champion, 1992 Tour DuPont stage winner. 77, 290, 301

Ernest Hemingway: Nobel Prize-winning author and war correspondent; works include *The Sun Also Rises, For Whom the Bell Tolls, A Moveable Feast* and others. 131, 137, 139, 211, 266

Greg Herbold: U.S. pro downhill mountain bike racer; national champion (1988-89, 1993); world champion (1990). 41, 70, 75, 76, 151, 163, 169, 187, 244, 250

Maynard Hershon: cycling writer 54

Roger Hertz: cycling advocate 318

Claude Herve: cycled around the world. 262

Stephane Heulot: French pro road racer; 1996 French national champion; Tour de France yellow jersey wearer (1996). 252, 257

Tom Hillard: mountain bike coach. 160, 194

Bernard Hinault: French pro road racer known as "The Badger" for his ferocious riding style; 5-time Tour de France winner (1978-79, 1981-82, 1985, including 28 stage wins and 77 days in the maillot jaune), 1986 Tour de France King of the Mountain leader, Vuelta a Espana (1978, 1983), Giro d'Italia (1980, 1982, 1985), world champion (1980), Ghent-Wevelgem (1977), Liege-Bastogne-Liege (1977, 1980), Paris-Roubaix (1981), Amstel Gold Race (1981), Grand Prix des Nations (1977-79, 1982), Fleche-Wallonne (1979, 1983), Tour of Lombardy (1979, 1984); only Eddy Merckx has greater palmares. 46, 83, 151, 153, 189, 192, 207, 234, 241, 253, 257

Eric Hjertberg: wheel designer and co-founder of Wheelsmith. 282, 284

Jon Hjertberg: wheel designer and co-founder of Wheelsmith. 282

Matt Hoffman: BMX freestyler. 163

Seana Hogan: 1993-1995 women's Race Across America winner. 186

Heidi Hopkins: U.S. racer. 63

Chris Horner: U.S. pro road racer. 252

Ray Hosler: cyclist. 263

Henry Beetle Hough: literary writer; author of *Singing in the Morning*. 50, 298-9

Allan Howard: bicycle patrolman in Dayton, Ohio. 313

John Howard: U.S. road racer; 1968 Olympic cycling team, 1971 Pan-American Games gold medalist (road race). 81, 274

Rune Hoydahl: Norwegian pro cross-country mountain bike racer. 93, 102

Dale Hughes: mountain bike organizer and NORBA board member. 42

Ralph Hurne: literary writer; author of *The Yellow Jersey*, generally acclaimed as the best novel about cycling. 60, 74, 121, 132, 141, 205, 217, 230, 231, 247

Aldous Huxley: novelist and critic; author of *Brave New World, Doors of Perception, Crome Yellow* and other works. 263

Miguel Indurain: Spanish pro road racer; 5-time Tour de France winner (1991-95), 2-time Giro d'Italia winner (1992-93); Paris-Nice (1989-90), World ITT Championship (1995), Olympic gold medalist (1996), Hour Record (53.040 km, 1994); only cyclist to win the

Tour de France 5 consecutive times; only the second man (after Eddy Merckx, 1972) to take Tour de France and hour record in the same year. 86, 147, 154, 209, 215, 217, 218, 234, 235, 236, 252

Josh Ivey: U.S. pro downhill mountain bike racer. 75

J. B. Jackson: outdoors writer, founder of *Landscape* magazine. 18

Gert Jakobs: pro road racer from the Netherlands. 149

Laurent Jalabert: French pro road racer; 1996 World Cup road champion, Vuelta a Espana (1995, 5 stage wins), 7 stage wins in 1994 Vuelta a Espana, Paris-Nice (1995-96), Milan-San Remo (1995), Fleche-Wallonne (1995), Criterium International (1995), Tour de France Points leader (1992, 1995); had reputation as a sprinter until he crashed out of the 1994 Tour de France, but came back in 1995 as a strong all-around rider. 108, 144, 214

Alfred Jarry: literary writer; author of *The Perpetual Motion Food Race.* 301

Jerome K. Jerome: literary writer and humorist; author of *Three Men in a Boat, Three Men on the Bummel* and other works. 52, 265, 284, 285, 335

Nicholas Johnson: journalist. 315

Philip Johnson: outdoors writer. 335

Steve Johnson: cycling coach. 105, 120

Uwe Johnson: literary writer; author of *The Third Book About Achim.* 52

Gareth Lovett Jones: cycling writer and photographer. 269

Mandible Jones: poet, author of *Carpet Particles* short story collection. 35, 205

Tinker Juarez: U.S. pro cross-country mountain bike racer; national champion (1994-95). 71, 147, 148, 204, 237

Bobby Julich: U.S. pro road racer. 65, 251

Shari Kain: U.S. pro mountain bike and cyclocross racer; 2-time national cyclocross champion (1994, 1996). 136

Yuri Kasirin: Russian cycling coach 111

Bob Katz: cycling advocate. 164

Mike Keefe: cycling writer and mechanic; author of The Ten Speed Commandments. 285

Charlie Kelly: cycling journalist and offroad pioneer who-along with Gary Fisher-coined the term "mountain bike." 32

Fred C. Kelly: journalist. 319

Sean Kelly: Irish pro road racer known as "The King of the Classics;" 7-time winner Paris-Nice (1982-88), 4-time Tour de France points leader (1982-83, 1985, 1989), Tour of Switzerland (1983), Tour of

Lombardy (1983, 1985, 1991), Paris-Roubaix (1984, 1986), Liege-Bastogne-Liege (1984, 1989), Milan-San Remo (1986, 1992), Grand Prix des Nations (1986), Ghent-Wevelgem (1988), Nissan Classic (1985-87, 1991), Vuelta a Espana (1988); 193 career wins; noted for being rather taciturn, Kelly once answered a question during a radio interview by nodding his head. 94

Andrew Kempe: founding member of the Orange County One Gear Club 169

John F. Kennedy: president of the United States (1961-1963). 25

Kent: French pop singer; composed a tune about Raymond Poulidor. 241

Ron Kiefel: U.S. pro road racer; Giro d'Italia stage winner (1986). 161, 193

Paul Kimmage: Irish pro road racer, author of *Rough Ride*. 61, 156, 235, 256

Betsy King: U.S. road racer and cycling coach; 5-time women's Tour de France rider (winner of 2 stages and climber's jerseys); multi-time national champion and World Cup winner. 58, 66

Mike King: U.S. pro downhill mountain bike racer; downhill world champion (1993). 75

Jan Kirstu: cycling coach 111

Rob Kish: U.S. ultramarathon road racer; winner of RAAM (1992, 1994-95). 223

Gerrie Knetemann: cycling coach and former road racer from the Netherlands; Amstel Gold Race (1974, 1985), world champion (1978). 207

Christopher Koch: cycling writer. 108, 125, 268, 336

Paul Koechli: Swiss pro road racer, team director and coach. 97

Dan Koeppel: cycling writer. 31, 34, 36, 139

Mike Kolin: cycling coach, author of Cycling for Sport. 86, 95

Charles Komanoff: cycling advocate. 313

Frank Kramer: 18-time U.S. national professional sprint champion. 99

Karl Kron: author of *Ten Thousand Miles on a Bicycle,* published in 1887. 48

Hennie Kuiper: pro road racer from the Netherlands; team director; Paris-Roubaix (1983), Milan-San Remo (1985), Tour of Flanders (1981), Tour of Lombardy (1981), world champion (1975). 220

Tom Kunich: cyclist 22

Atle Kvalsvoll: Norwegian pro road racer; noted climber. 63, 99

Chester Kyle: cycling aerodynamics expert. 276, 289

Jack Lambie: human-powered vehicle proponent, designer and engineer.

Mike McCarthy: U.S. racer who transformed himself from a road specialist to a world champion pursuit rider. 99

Frank McCormack: U.S. pro racer; national cyclocross champion (1996); Killington stage race champion (1995); Norwest Cup winner (1995); U.S. pro criterium champion (1995). 85

Lee McCormack: cycling writer. 33, 38

James McCullagh: cycling writer. 131

Seamus McGonagle: cycling writer and author of *The Bicycle in Life, Love, War and Literature.* 277

Jim McGurn: cycling writer and advocate; author of *On Your Bicycle.* 310

Marc Madiot: French pro road racer; 2-time winner of Paris-Roubaix (1985, 1992); team director. 251

Jason Makapagal: bicycle messenger. 195

Culzio Malaparte: cycling writer. 230

Laurence Malone: cycling writer; U. S. national road team member; mountain bike racer. 54, 150, 191

John Marino: U.S. ultramarathon road racer. 122

Butch Martin: cycling coach. 302

Doug Martin: GT Bicycles designer, team manager. 239, 280

Scott Martin: cycling writer. 51, 106

Miguel Martinez: French pro cross-country mountain bike racer. 95

Fred Matheny: cycling writer. 124, 290

Mark W. Matson: cyclist. 294

Ruthie Matthes: U.S. pro cross-country mountain bike racer; world champion (1991); World Cup champion (1992); national champion (1996). 162

Scott Matthews: bike commuter and endurance cyclist. 283

W. Somerset Maugham: English novelist and dramatist; author of *Of Human Bondage, Cakes and Ale* and other works. 51

Hiram Maxim: auto engineer for Albert Pope, first large-scale manufacturer of U.S. bicycles; author of *Horseless Days* (1937). 337

Eddy Merckx: Belgian pro road racer known as "The Cannibal," and almost unanimously considered the world's greatest cyclist ever; 525 career victories; 5-time Tour de France winner (1969-72, 1974), 5-time Giro d'Italia winner (1968, 1970, 1972-74), 3-time world champion (1967, 1971, 1974), Vuelta a Espana winner (1973), 3-time Paris-Nice winner (1969-71), Tour of Switzerland (1974), 7-time Milan-San Remo winner (1966-67, 1969, 1971-72, 1975-76), Ghent-Wevelgem (1967, 1969-70, 1973), Fleche-Wallonne (1967,

1970, 1972, 1975), Liege-Bastogne-Liege (1969, 1971-73, 1975), Paris-Roubaix (1968, 1970, 1973), Tour of Flanders (1969,1975), Tour of Lombardy (1971-72), Paris-Brussels (1973); hour record (49.432 km, 1972-84); only cyclist to win Tour de France, Giro d'Italia, Vuelta a Espana and Tour of Switzerland; one of two cyclists (with Stephen Roche) to win Tour de France, Giro d'Italia and world championship in same year (1970); one of two cyclists (with Miguel Indurain) to take Tour de France and hour record in same year (1972); in 1969, Merckx won all three major classifications (overall, points, and King of the Mountain) of the Tour de France. 44, 98, 100, 126, 147, 191, 209, 215, 220, 221, 227, 228, 232-35, 245, 246, 302

Robert Millar: British pro road racer; 11-time Tour de France rider; noted climber. 63, 189

Henry Miller: author of *Tropic of Cancer, Tropic of Capricorn, My Bike and Other Friends* and more. 15, 21, 24, 89

Keith Mills: cycling writer. 50, 313

Octave Mirbeau: journalist, novelist, literary critic, anarchist 178

Frederic Moncassin: French pro road racer; 1995 French national champion, Tour de France stage winner (1996). 284

William P. Morgan: sports psychologist. 106

Christopher Morley: literary writer; author of *The Romany Stain* (1926). 48, 178, 267, 299, 311

Pino Morroni: Italian cycling equipment and technical expert. 282

Francesco Moser: Italian pro road racer; hour record holder (50.151 km, 1984-1993), Giro d'Italia winner (1984), world champion (1977), Paris-Roubaix (1978-80), Milan-San Remo (1984), Tour of Lombardy (1975, 1978). 100-1, 148, 150, 257

George Mount: U.S. pro road racer; first American of modern era to race competitively at pro level in Europe. 238, 288, 329

Mark Mozer: amateur mountain biker and psychiatrist who raised 9 mountain-biking kids (including a pro and a U.S. junior national team rider). 178

Maurice de Muer: pro road racer. 208

Lisa Muhich: U.S. pro cross-country mountain bike racer; national champion (1987). 137

Owen Mulholland: cycling writer. 130, 238, 241

Jorg Muller: Swiss pro road racer; national champion. 104, 110

Louis Munger: highwheel racer and record holder; bike manufacturer; Major Taylor's coach/mentor. 110

Iris Murdoch: author of *The Sandcastle, The Red and the Green* and other works. 19

Johan Museeuw: Belgian pro road racer; World Cup winner (1995-96); world champion, winner of Paris-Roubaix (1996); national road champion (1992, 1996); Tour of Flanders (1993); two stage wins at Tour de France (1990). 46, 149, 224

Vladimir Nabokov: literary writer; author of *Lolita, Mary* and other works. 50

William Nealy: outdoors cartoonist, writer, humorist and adventurer; author of *Mountain Bike!* and *The Mountain Bike Way of Knowledge.* 189, 279.

Mike Neel: U.S. road racer; cycling coach. 93, 102, 104

Nancy Neely: track racer. 120

Scot Nicol: founder of Ibis Cycles; exquisite framebuilder. 40

Leonard Harvey Nitz: U.S. Olympic track racer. 106, 149

Marty Nothstein: U.S. track racer; world champion in match sprint and keirin (1994); Olympic silver medal in match sprint (1996). 166

Bill Nye: star of "Bill Nye: The Science Guy" educational TV show. 312

Alex Obbard: cyclist 294

Gene Oberpriller: U.S. pro cross-country mountain bike racer. 133

Graeme Obree: Scottish track racer; 2-time hour record holder (51.596 km, 1993), (52.713 km, 1994). 221

Flann O'Brien: literary writer; author of *The Third Policeman, The Dalkey Archive* and other works. 20, 279, 295, 297, 298

Sean O'Faolain: literary writer; author of *The Man Who Invented Sin and Other Stories.* 266

John Olsen: cycling writer; acoustics engineer; old-school trials rider. 34, 194, 238

Shaquille O'Neal: pro basketball star. 95

Mzee Opesen: recreational rider from Kampala, India. 165

Jake Orness: U.S. mountain bike racer. 252

P. J. O'Rourke: journalist and humorist. 334, 336

Ned Overend: U.S. pro cross-country mountain bike racer; 6-time national champion (1986-87, 1989-1992); world champion (1990); legendary for winning first-ever mountain bike world championships and competing through 1996 before retiring at the age of forty-one. 32, 39, 77, 97, 112, 130, 133, 136, 139, 140, 152, 198, 204, 237, 238, 283

Shaun Palmer: U.S. pro downhill mountain biker racer. 95

Marco Pantani: Italian pro road racer; 2-time Tour de France stage winner (1995), including l'Alpe d'Huez; 3rd overall Tour de France (1994), 2nd overall Giro d'Italia (1994); climbing specialist. 46, 73, 163

John Parker: mountain bike designer and builder. 237

Stewart Parker: playwright whose works include *Spokesong*. 25, 274, 276

Thom Parks: cyclist, environmentalist. 268

Ed Pavelka: cycling writer; winner of age-division team RAAM. 118

Simon Peat: recreational cyclist, European cycling advocate 274

Per Pedersen: pro road racer from Denmark. 216

Allan Peiper: Australian pro road racer 254

Henri Pelissier: French pro road racer; Paris-Brussels, Paris-Roubaix, Bourdeaux-Paris, Milan-San Remo 61, 214, 243

Dave Pelletier: cyclist and race organizer 225

Robert W. Pelton: author of *The Complete Book of Voodoo* 303

Nelson Pena: cycling writer 123

Andrea Peron: Italian pro road racer 137

Grant Petersen: product manager of Bridgestone Cycles, founder of Rivendell Bicycle Works; term "retrogrouch" was coined in reference to his cycling preferences 19, 255, 275

Len Pettyjohn: U.S. cycling coach and team director 111

Paola Pezzo: Italian pro cross-country mountain bike racer; first mountain bike Olympic gold medalist (1996); world champion (1993); European champion (1994) 200

Michelle Pfeiffer: actress 286

Jacquie Phelan: U.S. pro mountain biker racer, coach and founder of the Women's Mountain Bike and Tea Society (WOMBATS); 3-time national champion (1983-85); spouse of Charlie Cunningham 41, 64, 138, 155, 162, 185, 328

Davis Phinney: U.S. pro road racer; national pro road champion (1991); Olympic team time trial bronze (1984); first American to win a stage of Tour de France (1986); Coors Classic winner (1988); accomplished sprinter; spouse of Connie Carpenter 86, 87, 88, 98, 191

Pablo Picasso: artist 293, 299

Pineapple Bob: U.S. cyclist and off-road riding icon 137

Romano Pisi: bike expert at Bianchi 281

Jean-Paul van Poppel: pro road racer from the Netherlands 88, 125, 208

Raymond Poulidor: French pro road racer known as "The Eternal Second" for his near-misses; won Milan-San Remo (1961) 10, 153, 229, 241, 256

Daryl Price: U.S. pro cross-country mountain bike racer 133, 239

Jane Quigley: U.S. track racer; 10-time national champion; 7-time world champion medalist 150

Marie Louise de la Ramee: novelist; works include *Held in Bondage, Puck, The Ugliness of Modern Life* and others 333

Greg Randolph: U.S. pro road and mountain bike racer 169

James Reaney: poet; works include *Twelve Letters to a Small Town* 22

John Reed: journalist and poet; works include *Red Russia, Ten Days that Shook the World* and others 301

Mary Jane (Miji) Reoch: U.S. road racer; 11-time national road and track champion, 1975 world pursuit silver medal; cycling coach 98, 330

Hans Rey: Swiss trials rider and stunt-riding media sensation 161, 166, 238

Pascal Richard: Swiss pro road racer; Tour de France stage winner (1996), Liege-Bastogne-Liege (1996), 1996 Olympic road race silver medalist (road race) 215

Bjarne Riis: Danish national road champion; 1996 Tour de France winner, including 2 stage wins. 95, 154, 189, 241, 252

Stephen Roche: Irish pro road racer; Giro d'Italia (1987), Tour de France (1987), world champion (1987), Paris-Nice (1981); won the Giro, Tour and world championship in 1987, repeating a feat only Eddy Merckx had accomplished previously 23, 61, 152, 195, 220, 221, 242, 243, 250, 253

Myles Rockwell: U.S. pro downhill mountain bike racer; winner of Reebok Eliminator (1993) 32, 70, 83, 99, 138, 163, 202

Chepe Rodriguez: Colombian pro road racer; winner of 1996 Tour de France stage 257

Thurlow Rogers: U.S. pro road racer 53, 123

Gabriele Rolin: cycling writer 133

Bob Roll: U.S. pro road and cross-country mountain bike racer; freaky personality and author of *Bobke: A Ride on the Wild Side of Cycling* 82, 185, 190, 216, 237, 242

Franck Roman: pro mountain bike downhill racer from France 71, 187

Tony Rominger: Swiss pro road racer; 3-time Vuelta a Espana winner (1992-94), Giro d'Italia (1995), Tour de France King of Mountain and 2nd overall (1993); hour record (55.291 km, 1994). 105, 109, 165, 203, 222

Doug Roosa: cycling writer 279, 281

Teho de Rooy: pro road racer 220

Gerard Rue: French pro road racer; equipier (super domestique) 155, 235

Charles Ruys: Australian coach, manager and race promoter 151, 192

Wolfgang Sachs: late 1890s–early 1900s auto engineer; author of *For Love of the Automobile* 302

Carl Sagan: astrophysicist with a funny speech pattern 300

William Saroyan: literary writer; author of *The Daring Young Man on the Flying Trapeze, The Human Comedy, The Bicycle Rider in Beverly Hills* and others 18, 25, 48, 181,264,271,300, 302, 338

Jean-Paul Sartre: existential philosopher, dramatist, and author; works include *Being and Nothingness,* and others 296

Eddy Schepers: Belgian pro road racer; equipier (super domestique) 138, 152, 195

John Scherwa: newspaper sports editor and writer 338

Max Sciandri: British pro road racer; 1996 Olympic road race bronze medalist, Leeds International Classic (1995) 192, 256

Dave Scott: triathlete; multiple winner of Ironman triathlon 94

Bob Seals: originator of the Cool Tool, and Retrotec mountain bike that resembles old-style cruisers 42, 278

Kathy Sessler: 1992 and 1993 veteran U.S. national downhill mountain bike champion 121, 140, 167, 327

Ross Shafer: founder of Salsa bike company 39

George Bernard Shaw: literary writer, playwright, author of *Back to Methuselah* 177, 331

George Sheehan: essayist; running journalist 23

Jeff Shmoorkoff: U.S. randonneur (long-distance cycling event) 186

Andrew Shrimpton: cycling writer 311

Tom Shuler: U.S. pro road racer; cycling coach and team director 289

Alan Sillitoe: literary writer; author of "The Bike" and *Loneliness of the Long-Distance Runner 83, 265*

Tom Simpson: British pro road racer; world champion (1965), Paris-Nice (1967); died on Mont Ventoux during 1967 Tour de France 168

Andrew E. Slough: cycling writer 124

Matt Smith: U.S. mountain bike racer 11

Robert Smith: author of *A Social History of the Bicycle* 326

Ted Smith: first American to compete in world pro road race championship (1950) 156

John Stamstad: U.S. mountain bike endurance racer; 3-time winner of Iditabike, Leadville Trail 100, Montezuma's revenge; off-road 24-hour record (287 miles) 135, 203

Rich Stark: U.S. ultramarathon racer 208

James E. Starrs: editor of *The Noiseless Tenor,* a compilation of literary excerpts that involve cycling, republished in paperback by

Breakaway Books as *The Literary Cyclist*   24, 51, 55, 121, 176, 262, 264, 265, 267, 269, 270, 294, 297, 299, 311, 314, 318

Rik van Steenbergen: Belgian pro road racer; Tour of Flanders (1944, 1946), Paris-Roubaix (1948, 1952), Fleche-Wallonne (1949, 1958), Paris-Brussels (1950), Milan-San Remo (1954), 3-time world champion (1949, 1956-57); 40 victories in 6-day races 110, 232

Gloria Steinem: feminist and founder of *Ms.* magazine 305

Neil Stephens: Australian pro road racer; equipier (super domestique) 194, 195, 209, 267

Alex Stieda: Canadian pro road racer; first North American to wear Tour de France's yellow jersey 104

David Story: cyclist 286

Rob Story: cycling writer 43, 264

Marla Streb: U.S. pro downhill and cross-country mountain bike racer

Fred Streibeigh: cyclist 163, 203, 266, 305, 327

Donald Sutherland: expert bike mechanic; author of the indispensable *Sutherland's Handbook for Bicycle Mechanics* 287

Dick Swann: cycling historian 50

Alison Sydor: Canadian pro cross-country mountain bike racer; silver medalist at first Olympic mountain bike race, World Cup champion (1996) 37, 42, 65, 132, 144, 188

Glenn Temml: cyclist who pedaled the Daedalus Project into flight 303

John Tesh: TV commentator; composer of "Tour de France" and "Tour de France: The Early Years" music albums 218

Steve Tesich: screenwriter whose credits include *Breaking Away* 49

Bernard Thevenet: French pro road racer; winner of Tour de France (1975, 1977) 167, 208

Dietrich Thurau: German world champion track racer 112, 257

Steve Tilford: U.S. pro cross-country mountain bike racer; national champion (1983) 120

John Tomac: U.S. pro cross-country and downhill mountain bike racer; national cross-country champion (1988, 1996); national downhill champion (1991, 1994); cross-country world and World Cup champion (1991) 9, 35, 37, 71-3, 75, 96, 98, 110, 134, 239, 277

Lesley Tomlinson: Canadian pro cross-country mountain bike racer 250

Pavel Tonkov: Russian pro road racer; won Giro d'Italia (1996) and Tour of Switzerland (1995) 146

Leon Trotsky: Russian revolutionary 319

Harry S. Truman: U.S. president (1945-53) 305

Ken Turan: movie critic 173

Mark Twain: literary writer; humorist; author of *The Adventures of Huck Finn, Tom Sawyer, A Connecticut Yankee in King Arthur's Court,* the essay, "Taming the Bicycle," and other works 65, 127, 162, 174, 178

Rebecca Twigg: U.S. road and track racer; Olympic silver (1984 road) and bronze (1992 individual pursuit); 6-time individual pursuit world champion (1982, 1984-85, 1987, 1993, 1995); 16-time national champion; 3-time winner of Ore-Ida Women's Challenge road race 143

Nelson Vails: U.S. track racer; Olympic match sprint silver (1984) 143, 254

Richard Virenque: French pro road racer; 3-time Tour de France King of Mountain leader (1994-96) 46, 61, 65, 146, 201, 204

Nicolas Vouilloz: French pro downhill mountain bike racer; 2-time world champion (1995-96); 2-time World Cup winner (1995-96); European champion (1994) 119

Mike Walden: cycling coach 100

David Walsh: cycling writer 64, 87, 233

Bobby Walthour, Jr.: U.S. track racer; national champion (1921) 283

Carol Waters: U.S. mountain bike racer; 1992 world champion veteran cross-country mountain bike racer 101, 106, 326, 328

Jake Watson: U.S. pro downhill mountain bike racer; nicknamed "Earthquake" 75, 188

Amy Webster: bike messenger 164

Bob Weir: Grateful Dead guitarist 304

John Weissenrider: U.S. pro cross-country mountain bike racer 302

H. G. Wells: literary writer; author of *The Time Machine, The War of the Worlds, The Island of Doctor Moreau, The Wheels of Chance* (his cycling novel) and other works; an avid cyclist 18, 79, 171, 174, 178, 179, 305

Elizabeth West: author of *Hovel in the Hills, Garden in the Hills* and other works 19

Michael White: U.S. track and road racer; 12-hour world record holder

Cindy Whitehead: U.S. pro cross-country and downhill mountain bike racer; national cross-country champion (1986); national downhill champion (1990) 327

W. C. Whitney: U.S. Naval Secretary, 1896 318

Dave Wiens: U.S. pro cross-country mountain bike racer; national champion (1993); designer of first Olympic mountain bike course (1996); spouse of Susan DeMattei 103, 284

Frances Willard: 19th-century feminist; author of *How I Learned to Ride the Bicycle* 82, 162, 174-6, 197, 294, 295, 307

Paul Willerton: U.S. pro mountain bike and road racer 37, 137

Sloan Wilson: journalist 175

Stuart S. Wilson: journalist 18, 274, 316

Tom Winter: cyclist 38

Gary Wockner: cycling writer; author of *Gold Hill and Back* and *Sex With a Mountain Bike* 268

Frosty Woolridge: cyclist 270

Steve Woznik: U.S. road bike racer 204

Brock Yates: automobile journalist 334

Roger Yates: Sean's dad 131

Sean Yates: British pro road racer considered one of the all-time great domestiques and descenders; Tour de France stage winner (1988), Tour de France maillot jaune wearer (1994, 1 day) 68, 118, 148, 216, 242

John William Yope: poet 325

Connie Young: U.S. track racer; 4-time match sprint world champion (1982-84, 1990); 9-time match sprint national champion (1982-83, 1985, 1987-89, 1992, 1994-95) 123, 193

Roger Young: U.S. track racer; 1973 national sprint champion, 1975 Pan-Am Games team pursuit gold; cycling coach 107

Lennard Zinn: cycling writer; bike designer and builder 265, 294

Dino Zandegu: pro road racer 240

Alex Zulle: Swiss pro road racer; Vuelta a Espana (1996), Tour de France maillot jaune wearer (1992, 1996), Tour de France Prologue winner (1996), Paris-Nice (1993) 148, 155